# LACE not lace

## Contemporary Fiber Art from Lacemaking Techniques

Devon Thein

Hunterdon Art Museum

Openwork Imprint

Published in conjunction with the exhibition
Lace, not Lace: Contemporary Fiber Art from Lacemaking Techniques

Hunterdon Art Museum, Clinton, New Jersey
Sept 23, 2018 — Jan 6, 2019

Design: Kathleen Collins, Openwork Imprint



IBSN: 978-1-7326224-0-1

Editors: Elena Kanagy-Loux, Amy Mills and Nancy Neff

Illustrations: Elena Kanagy-Loux

Front Cover: Penny Nickels, *The Jersey Devil*
Design: Kathleen Collins

# Contents

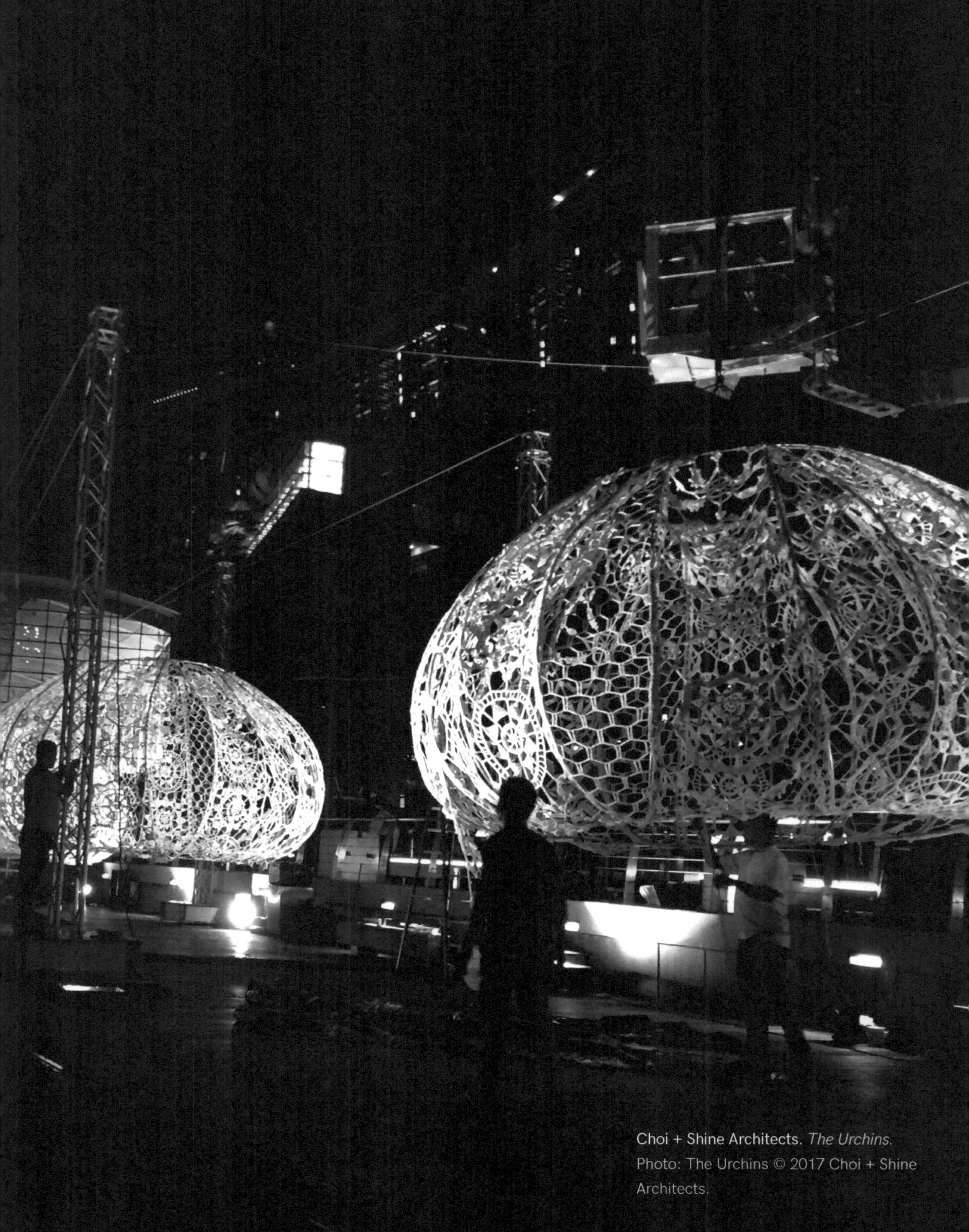

Choi + Shine Architects. *The Urchins.*
Photo: The Urchins © 2017 Choi + Shine Architects.

# Acknowledgements

Handmade lace as a medium for contemporary art has been neglected by museums. For most of us who make decisions about exhibitions, it barely has been on our radar screens. Contemporary exhibitions that have focused on lace have more often than not included objects that are steel or glass with patterns of holes rather than objects made of bobbin or needle lace. How fortunate that my husband, a mathematician, returned to our hotel room in Vancouver after a day at a mathematics conference to tell me that he had met someone that I might find interesting, a mathematician, Veronika Irvine, who creates lace patterns. Later that week, sharing a taxi to the airport, she showed me images on her cell phone. I came back to the Hunterdon Art Museum eager to propose a contemporary lace exhibition. My thanks to Veronika for planting the seed.

Serendipity followed me as I searched for a lace expert to be HAM's guest curator. Three thousand miles from where I met Veronika, Devon Thein, whose home in New Jersey is fifteen minutes from mine, answered the call. Devon, whose interest in and knowledge of lace, both contemporary and historic, seem inexhaustible, was a curator of the Metropolitan Museum of Art's exhibition *Gems of European Lace, ca. 1600 – 1920*, has written many articles about lace, and is a lacemaker. Known internationally by the lace community, Devon was a perfect fit. She has put together a phenomenal group of artworks by 28 artists of eleven nationalities. My thanks go to Devon for not only creating a beautiful show that represents a broad range of contemporary lacemaking, but also for her willingness to reach out to the lace world to help support the exhibition and for envisioning a catalog worthy of the exhibition. My appreciation is also extended to Kathleen Collins, Elena Kanagy-Loux, Amy Mills, and Nancy Neff for their work on this publication.

The lace community has been overwhelmingly generous in their support of Lace, not Lace. On behalf of Hunterdon Art Museum's Board of Trustees and staff, I thank the International Organization of Lace, Inc. as well as the many lace groups and individuals whose donations have helped make this show possible. Additionally, we are grateful to the lenders to the exhibition.

My deep appreciation goes to the Coby Foundation, Ltd., which specializes in the textile and needle arts, and its executive director Ward L. E. Mintz for the Foundation's very generous support of the exhibition. Over the years, the Foundation's significant generosity has been important to HAM's exhibition program, which has included many fiber shows.

As always we are grateful for the continuing support of the New Jersey State Council on the Arts and the Geraldine R. Dodge Foundation, whose general operating support is critical to HAM's existence.

HAM's staff and volunteers are extraordinary. My thanks to our Exhibitions Coordinator Ellen Maher as well as Jennifer Brazel, Michael Citarelli, Erin Delgado, Joan Gavornik, Dave Harding, Donna Huron, and Mary Ellen O'Neal along with Ingrid Renard, Ellen Siegel and the installation crew. Special thanks to Bill Ivie of Cinematiceye and Dana Lane.

Most importantly, we extend our gratitude and thanks to the artists whose work is on display in this exhibition. We are in awe of their creativity and skill.

Marjorie Frankel Nathanson
Executive Director

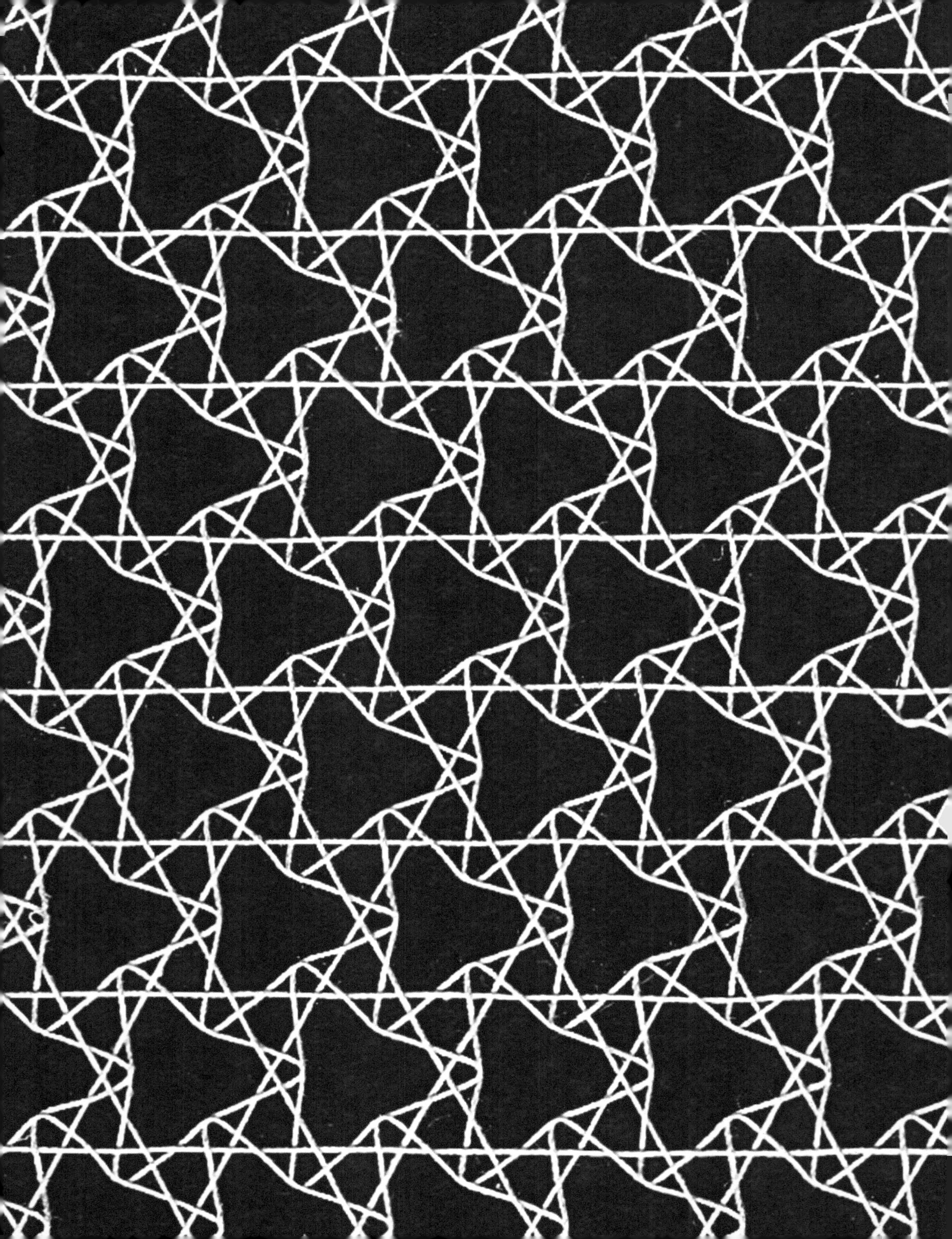

## Curatorial Acknowledgements

I would like to thank the Hunterdon Art Museum for seeing the value in holding an exhibit of lace art. Many thanks to Director Marjorie Frankel Nathanson for her indefatigable efforts to put on this exhibit and to her cheerful and professional staff who were a pleasure to work with. Thanks, as well, to the Coby Foundation, Ltd. for its significant financial support. I am indebted to all the artists and collectors who were so obliging and patient with me throughout this process and who so generously shared their art.

Words cannot express my gratitude to Kathleen Collins of Openwork Imprint for her impressive skills and unfaltering perseverance in producing this catalog. Thanks also to the all-volunteer editorial staff, Elena Kanagy-Loux, Amy Mills and Nancy Neff . I am overwhelmed by their willingness to spend so much of their time making this catalog a success. I am grateful to Sarah Wilson and Gary Thein for their unflagging support and proofreading.

The exhibit could not have happened without the generous contribution of the International Organization of Lace, Inc., the donations of many local lace groups, and also of individual lacemakers. Special thanks as well to Gunnel Teitel, Jeri Ames and all the members of Arachne for allowing me to consult them. I am grateful to the lace community for the many years of friendship and camaraderie that we have enjoyed together. It has been a privilege to spend so much of my life with people who share my passion. I hope they will be pleased with this catalog and this exhibit.

Devon Thein
Curator

Veronika Irvine. *Triaxial Arrow Heads,* 2015,
White cotton thread on charcoal raw silk,
handmade bobbin lace, 12″ x 12″.

## Lace, not Lace: Contemporary Fiber Art from Lacemaking Techniques

Devon Thein

What is lace? Is it a white airy substance, or is it a textile made from the specially adapted techniques of needle lace and bobbin lace? This exhibit is intended to introduce the public to contemporary art made in needle and bobbin lace which may defy conventional expectations associated with the word "lace".

Weaving and looping are among the oldest techniques for building a textile, dating to prehistory. In the late 16th century, the demand for beautiful luxury textiles led to elaborating these ancient techniques into fiber art of enormous complexity and refinement to adorn the clothing of the aristocracy. The high value placed on neckwear, especially white neckwear, created a luxury industry that employed vast numbers of people, and that was constantly innovating along with rapidly changing fashions. It was in this hothouse of wealth and vanity that needle lace, a form of looping, and bobbin lace, a form of weaving, developed as the premier forms of textile production.

Needle lace is a fabric produced by making linked buttonhole stitches, one after another in different patterns, and configurations. It is embroidery without the fabric. Bobbin lace is a combination of braiding and weaving. It is weaving without a loom. There is no fixed warp. The threads, held on bobbins, can operate interchangeably as warp or weft allowing great versatility. The bobbin lacemaker can weave in any direction, even three dimensionally. Unlike loom weaving where the fabric is always a square or a rectangle, the bobbin lacemaker may choose to weave a textile in the shape of a unicorn or a flowerpot. These two fiber art techniques, quite dissimilar in practice, synchronized in appearance and use during the historical period when lace was center stage in the world of luxury apparel.

The fact that these techniques reached their apex to fulfill the need for largely white fashion accessories has created a sense of etymological confusion. Most people would say lace is something white with holes in it, whether produced by machine or in other techniques. Meanwhile the techniques of needle lace and bobbin lace are often used to produce textiles that are colored, or solid in appearance. Sometimes they are used with wire to produce jewelry. Many works in needle lace or bobbin lace techniques would not be recognized as lace by the public. "Where is the lace?" is a frequent comment when viewing contemporary lace.

To place lace fiber art in historical perspective, it is important to understand that when lace was a commercial industry, the women who made the lace never designed the lace. It was designed by professional designers, artists who specialized in decorative arts. It was sold for use in fashion and interior design; thus, it was subject to the same cost considerations of any commercial product. But, needle lace and bobbin lace are difficult to learn and slow to practice. As the cost of human labor became higher and the appearance of machine made lace improved, handmade lace lost the battle for its traditional market niche.

Although many mourned the passing of this industry, in fact, freedom from economic considerations resulted in creative freedom for lacemakers. The resurgence in lacemaking during the craft revival of the 1970s was among people who practiced it as a hobby, or artists who made art in the techniques. The 1970s saw an explosion of imaginative lacemaking as lacemakers were free to experiment with size and materials. Driven by the satisfaction of working in such fluid textile techniques, lacemakers of the late 20th century researched historical lace to fully explore and describe the almost unlimited tool box of skills, often publishing extraordinary books in limited runs.

Now, lacemaking is having another renaissance in popularity, as artists, who are often technologically sophisticated are drawn to these complicated, and very mathematical forms of textile production. Building on the foundation of the lace revival of the 1970s they are interpreting lace with the help of computers and 21st century fibers. Today's lace artists are interested in scientific subjects and philosophical questions posed by living in a highly technological society.

This exhibit at the Hunterdon Art Museum combines the work of the lace innovators of the late 20th century lace revival with the work of a younger generation of lacemakers. Twenty-eight artists, representing eleven nationalities are exhibiting their work in one place. This is the first exhibit in the United States to focus on art made in traditional lace techniques, which are largely unknown. It is intended to introduce the public and other artists to the strengths of bobbin and needle lace as creative media, and to inspire others to try them out.

Lenka Suchanek. *Are We Made of Lace?*, 2012.

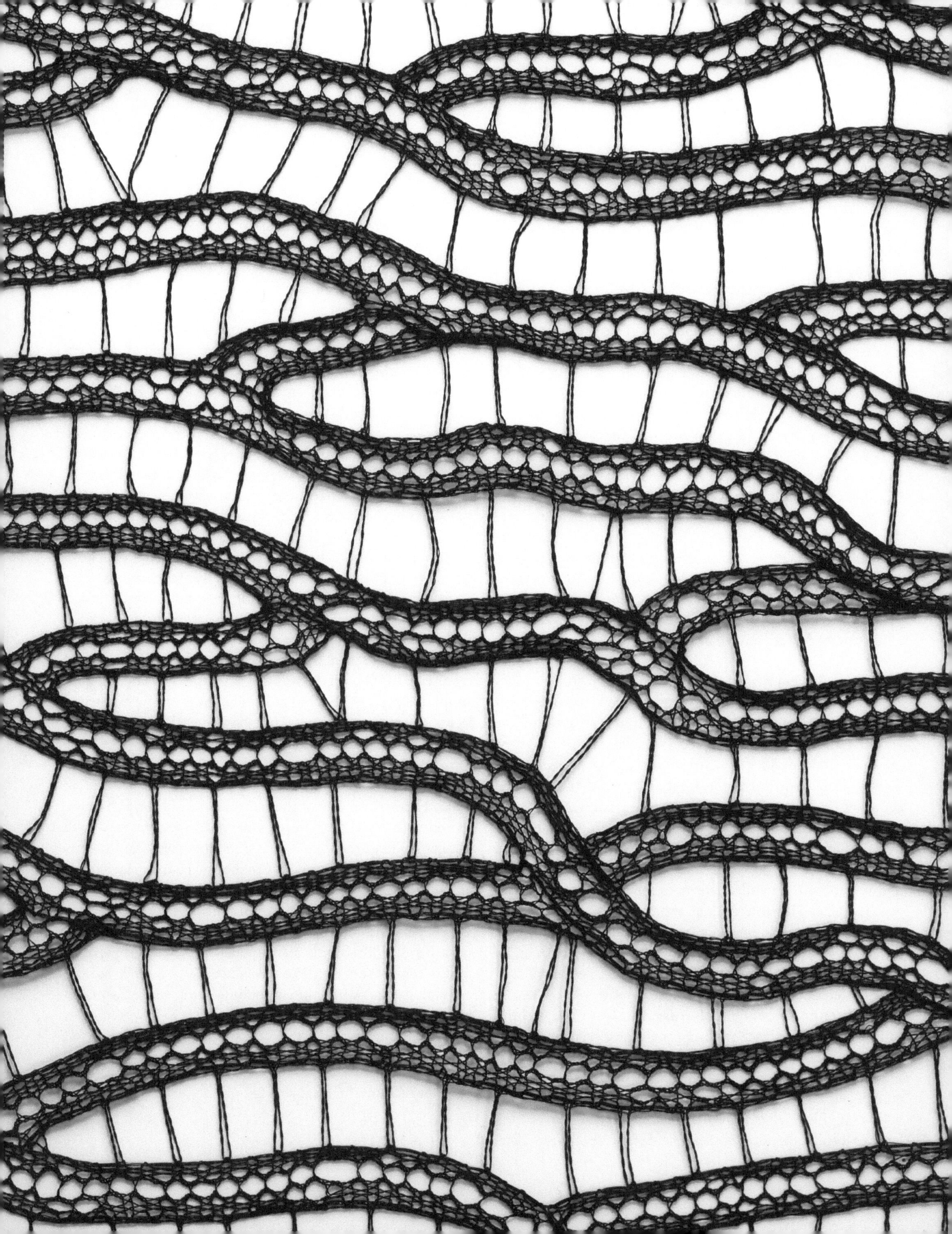

## Czech Contemporary Lace and Milča Eremiášová

Dagmar Beckel-Machyckova

I fell in love with lace in 1989. I was ten years old, and hiking though mountains in Slovakia (formerly Czechoslovakia) with my mother, when we walked into a village where ladies sat on front porches and made lace. I had never seen such a thing but was mesmerized and that night tried to repeat the motions with a few pens and thread I pulled out of my mother's travel sewing kit. That first lace I saw was Špania Dolina, in which a torchon-like grid precisely guides each fiber to its destination, each element repeated in regular intervals. I love the geometry and the logic of the craft: it clicks with the way my brain works and I thoroughly enjoy it.

In 1992, at a point when I had mastered the basics of bobbin lace, I attended an exhibition in the church of Saint Roch in Prague. A single artist, Milča Eremiášová, filled the entire 17th century church space with objects of fine art, three-dimensional structures and images in a technique that could easily be called paintings with fiber, so delicate were these masterpieces of lace. It was the first time I realized that bobbin lace had no limits. Years later I had the privilege of being one of Milča's students.

The Czech Lacemaking School is well known for its ability to create pieces that disrupt the status quo. But how is it possible that a straightforward and apparently rigid technique can create such phenomenal pieces and what helps make the leap? To understand it we must first start with geography. Czech Republic (formerly Czechoslovakia) lies in the center of Europe and as various emperors, commanders, and leaders stormed through the lands, they each brought their own influence--some from the East, some from the West. Tradesmen would go to market in a neighboring country and return with new ideas for patterns based on what they saw. The Czech lacemakers, eager to deliver their best, would quickly learn how to incorporate these ideas into their own patterns. Such influences can be traced into lace schools' curricula up through today. In America, lacemakers may learn different laces such as Milanese, Cluny or Idrija taking care to use the authentic tools, rules and historical designs. However, the Czech schools import all these techniques into their lace, subordinating them to the rules of Czech lace. This results in an extraordinarily rich toolbox of techniques enabling the Czech lacemakers' creativity. When combined with a highly sophisticated lace education system dating back to 1767, it is not surprising that the Czech lacemakers were able to create revolutionary pieces.

Czech (Czechoslovak) lace begins to be discussed in the early 1900s as a part of a nationalistic movement in Europe that looked to history and traditions for self-identification of individual nations. In 1908 ethnographers Regína Bíbová and Marie Smolková documented the many different regional laces worked in the geographic location of Czechoslovakia in a publication called *Lace and Lace-making of the Slavonic People in Bohemia, Moravia, Silesia, and Slovakia.*[1]

The shift to the contemporary Czechoslovak lace arrived on the heels of World War II, first with the establishment in 1946 of the Department of Lace and Embroidery at the Academy of Arts, Architecture, and Design in Prague. This department was active until 1959, when the founder, professor Emilie Paličková, retired. Professor Paličková brought a unique perspective into the lacemaking. Her ability to combine traditional folk art and modern design set a precedent for the following generations of fiber art designers as well as lacemakers. While she wowed the world in 1925 with a needle lace design *Sluníčko* (Sun) that required 11,000 hours to work, by 1946 she was encouraging simplified pieces in bobbin lace and a focus on the essence of lace with fewer techniques and motifs in each piece, until her designs reach an ingenious level of simplicity. Her methods were as unorthodox as her work.

Milča Eremiášová, one of the last students of Prof. Paličková, shared with me that the professor's favorite exercise was to ask her students to make figures in bobbin lace. The students had to wind bobbins first, then hang them on an empty pillow. There was no drawing, no pricking, just the threads and the vision of a human form in the student's head. Milča says it taught her a lot, and to this day she is able to work on a blank pillow, with just a pencil sketch nearby. Milča fondly remembers that Prof. Paličková was a quiet lady of a small stature, with high standards. She easily dismissed yards of completed work if she didn't find it to have sufficient artistic merit. Her highest praise was "this might do", thereby encouraging her students to push their limits and

Milča Eremiášová. Photo: Dagmar Beckel-Machyckova.

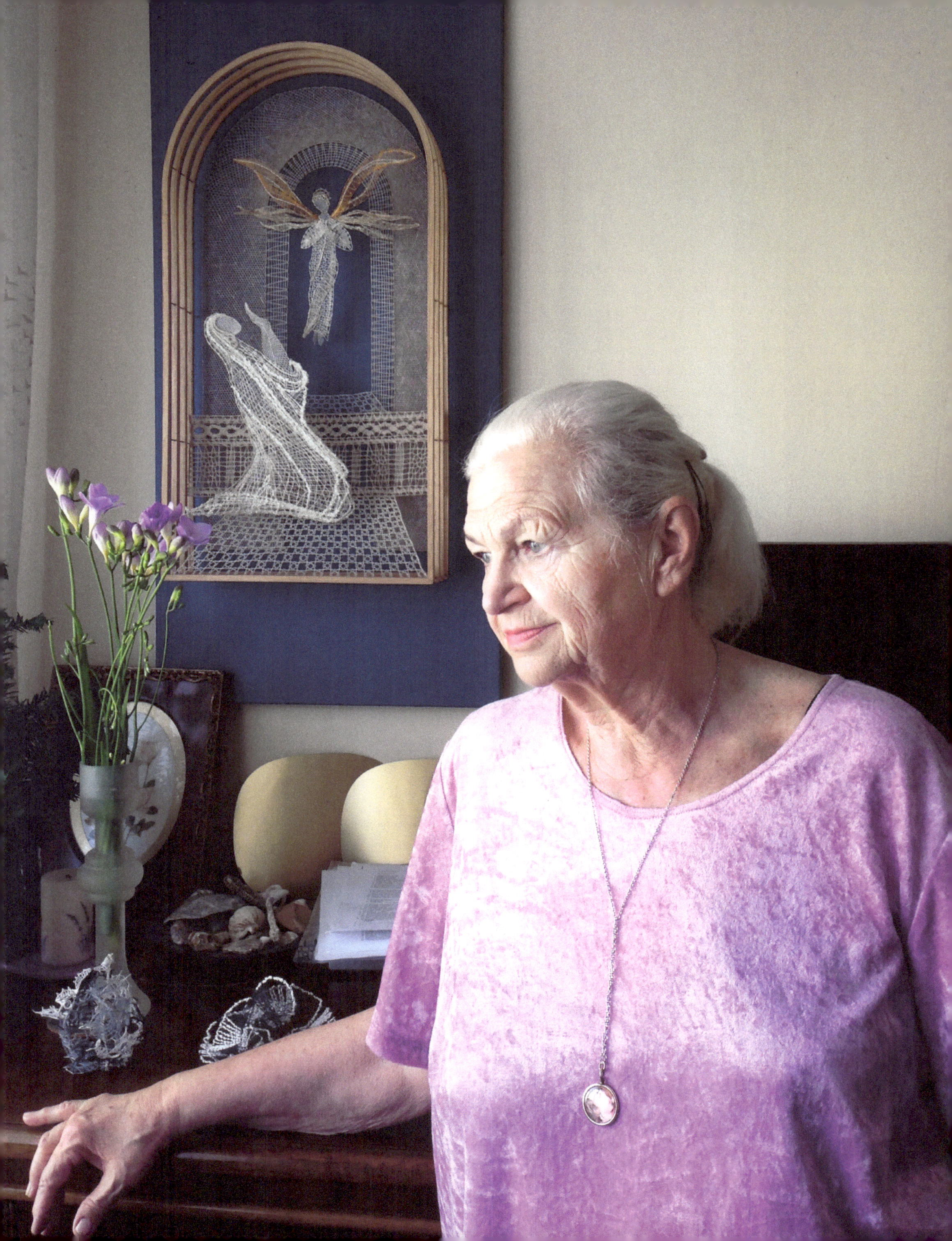

explore new possibilities. Her alumni include among others Eva Fialová, Vlasta Šolcová, Blanka Hanušová, and Marie Vaňková.

After Prof. Paličková retired in 1959 and the department closed, her students transitioned into the Department of Textile Design led by the director Antonín Kybal, a proponent of tapestry, who perceived lace as a textile with unique ability to capture light. He was instrumental in nudging contemporary lace into three-dimensional space, sometimes "cruelly crumpling" a finished piece of lace. Among his students were Milča Eremiášová, Emílie Frydecká, Ludmila Kaprasová, Marie Jarkovská, and others.

Prof. Kybal retired in 1970 and the Department thereafter produced textile artists focused on other than lacemaking techniques. The last generation of lacemakers to graduate from the Academy of Arts, Architecture and Design included Vlasta Wasserbauerová, Marianna Horváthová and Alina Jašková, in the late 1980s under the mentorship of Vlastimil Vodák. Following the fall of Communism in 1989, lace became less and less desirable in the emerging capitalistic economy, and with it disappeared the Master

Emílie Paličková. *Sluníčko (Sun)*, 1925. Photo: Éditions Albert Levy.

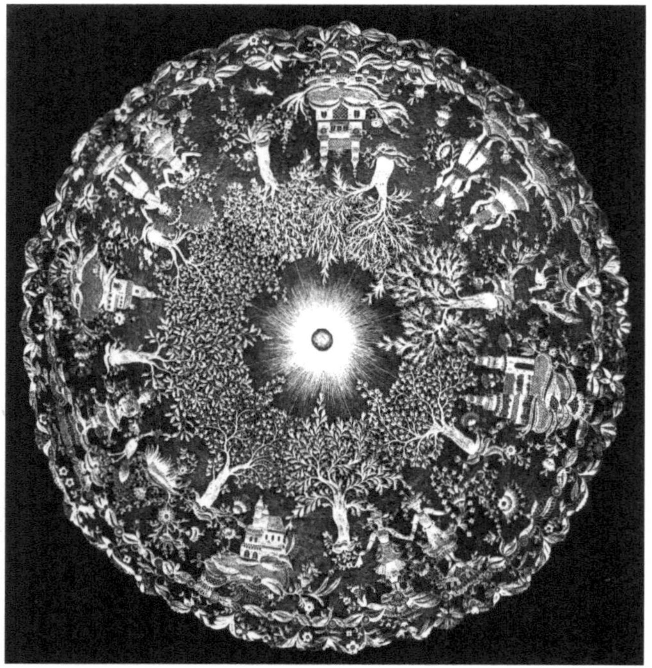

of Fine Arts in Lace degree. The Communistic structure of a centrally planned economy, while not necessarily advantageous to individual citizens, turned out to have been highly valuable for the art of lacemaking as it provided not only the education but more importantly guaranteed job openings in this industry.

In parallel with the post-WWII development of lace as an art form described above, the craft of lacemaking was promoted by the government. In 1948, following the presidential decrees banning private businesses, the Center for Folk Craft and Art Manufacturing, *"Ústředí lidové umělecké výroby"(ÚLUV)*, created satellite offices to unite the previously independent craftsmen in a collective. Their work was then designed by university trained artists who were also schooled in Czech folk culture.

One of these offices was called *"Vamberecká krajka"* (the lace of the Vamberk region). The structure of it was rather rigid because the centrally planned economy required each person to have a well-defined job. There was a planner working for the central office, who would decide what kinds of items needed to be created in the given year (i.e. the ratio of fashion accessories to interior design items, such as doilies or wall decor). He then submitted the plan to the designers at Vamberecká Krajka. The professional designers, graduates of the Academy of Arts, Architecture and Design, would create designs and pass them onto a "technical development lacemaker".

The "technical development lacemaker" had the responsibility of converting the designer's idea into a piece of lace. Her job was to document stitches and instructions, and to modify the design in a way that would make the piece easier to make while remaining technically accurate. Technique was something that was greatly emphasized and can be interpreted as doing things "the right way", meaning the way the state's lace school system would typically teach items such as transitions and finishes. A new technical drawing (the final pricking) would then be completed prior to being sent to the "common lacemakers".

When a "common lacemaker" received a job, it typically included an image or a finished sample completed by the "technical development lacemaker", and instructions (with various levels of detail). Each job specification also included the number of pieces to be made. For example, a Christmas ornament would need to be done 25 times in gold and 25 times in silver. The lacemaker would also receive an exactly allocated amount of thread for the job assigned, in this case the silver and gold. Should she run short an explanation was expected. The lacemaker took these supplies home and worked under a deadline. The pay was a set hourly rate, dependent solely on the time that the "technical developmental lacemaker" estimated it would take the piece to be finished. As money per piece was calculated by multiplying the set hourly rate by the estimated time it should take to complete it, this arrangement often put younger and less experienced lacemakers at a disadvantage. An oversight on the side of the developmental lacemaker easily compromised someone else's living.

This strict structure and need for industrial efficiency had the undesirable side effect of creating somewhat rigid designs. As Milča herself describes it, she was once approached by Vamberecká Krajka to design several pieces. Some months after submission, she saw a vaguely familiar lace in the store's window, and although she knew it was a piece she designed, she was surprised by how many changes were done to it. Instead of smooth fluid outlines and her characteristic poetic style of drawing, the system had created a geometrically accurate and precise design that lost all of its liveliness. It was the last time Milča designed for the Center, choosing instead to design and make her own bobbin lace art.

While all lace designers understood the lacemaking process, they did not always make their own lace, especially when it came to exhibition pieces. Often, a very experienced lacemaker worked closely with a designer and developed a relationship that required very little explicit instructions. Often designers whose names we are familiar with from large international shows, such as *Expo 58* and *Expo 67*, had an entire team of nameless lacemakers assigned to them. As Martina Rejzlová remembers, her mother (Jana Štefková) was the lacemaker who created most of Vaňková-Kuchyňková's objects. Often, her mother would have another lacemaker come stay overnight at her house and the two of them would sit side by side at an oversized pillow and work long hours to prepare a large exhibition piece.

But not all designers required a personal lacemaker. While working on the highly awarded lace exhibition *Expo 67* in Montreal, Prof. Kybal called all the designers into a room and laid out his design of the exhibit. Then he explained how many flowers, dresses and other pieces were necessary. The designers raised their hands and committed to what they

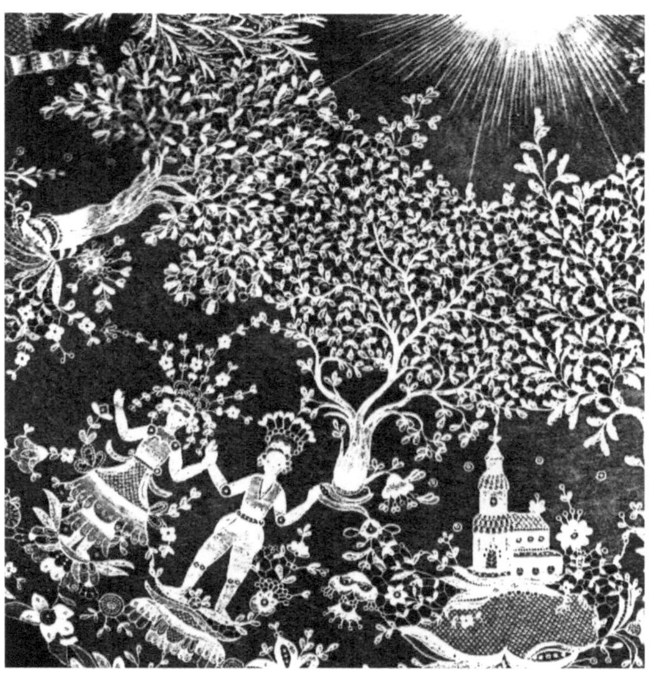

Emílie Paličková. *Sluníčko (Sun)*, 1925. Photo: Éditions Albert Levy.

could do. The next question was "do you need lacemakers to do it?" The Center would then assign the lacemakers to complete the work. Those designers that choose to do their work themselves were left to their own resources. Milča, for example, chose to decline those services as she preferred to make her own lace and feel the thread on the pillow.

Such highly specialized roles limited the ability to move effectively between lacemaker and designer roles. While working on someone else's designs certainly gives you practice, it also boxes you into that designer's style. One of the "personal" lacemakers explained to me that, after the Berlin Wall came down and the Institute closed, she decided to branch out on her own. It then took her years to become a designer in her own right, because initially her own designs looked the way her designer would have done it—gaining the independence and finding her own voice took years.

Milča's own life reflected the highs and lows of the Czechoslovak lace. She studied with Prof. Paličková only to transition to Kybal's studio, where she gained international acclaim as her work was recognized in both *Expo 58* and *Expo 67* exhibitions. Then political circumstances changed everything. The arrival of Russian soldiers in August of 1968 was followed by years of politically motivated "cleansing" that removed many progressively minded individuals, including Mr. Kybal. In an environment that rewarded individuals with peasant backgrounds, Milča Eremiášová, from a highly educated family that didn't support communism, was fortunate to find a teaching position as an art history teacher at the School Institute of Art Manufacturing until the early 1990s. After the fall of the Iron Curtain, the Czech Ministry of Education dismantled ÚLUV as undesirable and unnecessary. This was followed by closing the School Institute of Art Manufacturing (ŠÚUV), effectively crumbling the entire lace educational system and its marketing arm.

With the new economy came new opportunities, however. In 1992 Milča was offered a Department Director position at a newly formed private university. Alas, this was short lived--Milča left five years later. As was common in the 90's in a country with a free educational system, parents at a pay-for-college demanded their children pass their classes rather than learn the arts. To fill the void of closed schools and ÚLUV, private groups and co-ops began to sprout with the most significant of them based around two magazines Paličkování (Iva Prošková) and Krajka (Anička Halíková). Paličkování grew beyond a magazine and into a non- profit organization (Vzdělávací Spolek Uměleckých Řemesel) that united excellent teachers offering night and weekend classes. In this program Milča offered design classes to students, who mostly pursued lace as a hobby. She says that teaching is as important to her as lacemaking; even though she is retired, twice a year she meets with a small group of students.

Milča, who is celebrating her 80th birthday this year, represents a generation of lacemakers unlike any other. Professionally educated, their works shattered boundaries and elevated the craft into an art form. These works are now part of the permanent exhibition of the Vamberk lace museum, which showcases the masterpieces of 20th century Czech contemporary lace. In 2002 the museum started organizing a biennial juried exhibition of bobbin lace (Biennále české krajky) in order to support future development of lace, create technological advances in lacemaking, and to continue setting a high standard for Czech lacemakers. It is of interest that many of the winners in 2017 were well-known names associated with the original lace and textile program at the Academy of Arts, Architecture and Design. ∷

Milča Eremiášová. *Gothic Window,* 2015. Bobbin lace, cotton, 5″ x 10″. Photo: Dagmar Beckel-Machyckova.

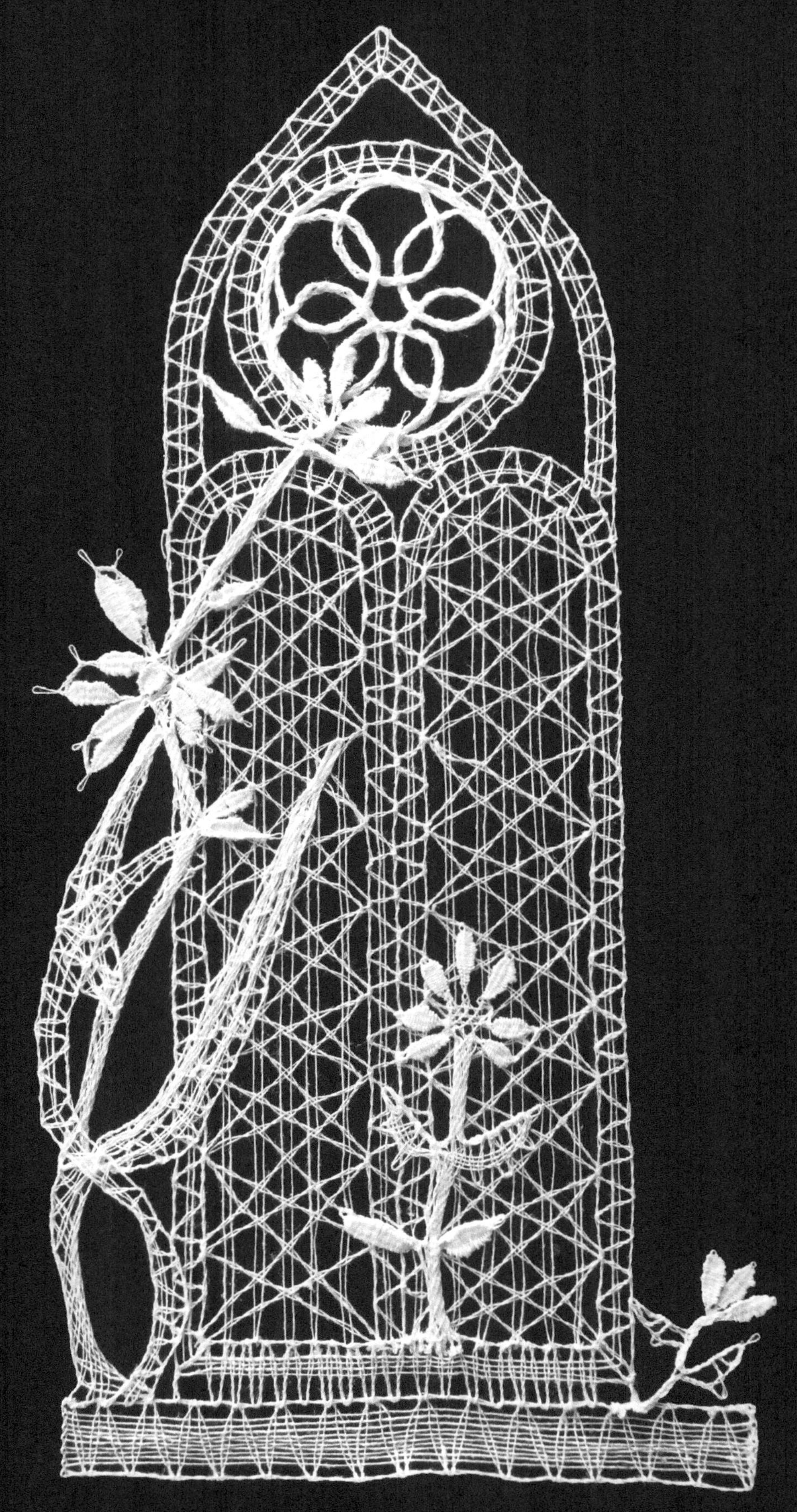

## The Carriage of Lost Love 1977 - 2018

Lieve Jerger

My childhood was blessed from the start. Almost every year, my parents Berthilda C. Vandoren and Marcel C. Baekelmans gave me a new sibling. Twice they came two-at-a-time. By age 12, I was the elder of a small tribe: Bruno, Herlinde (Spahr), Lucas, Lutgart, Christiaan, Ivo, Peter, Vera and Bert. It was like growing up in a great hall of mirrors. My family gave me plenty of love but also constant teasing and critique. Today, I am deeply grateful that I have so many brothers and sisters who keep me humble.

When Lucas ended his life at age 21, it was because of a broken heart, and it affected all of us profoundly and permanently. In the wake of this tragedy, my mother took up bobbin lacemaking which evolved into a lasting passion. She collected all the oldest handmade laces she could find in Antwerp and Bruges antique shops and assembled her *Spieghel Lace Collection*--over a thousand pieces of exquisitely handmade laces, some dating back as far as the 1500s. This collection has been the greatest inspiration for my own copper lace art.

Based on her research and her own textile treasures, she wrote *The Mirror of Lace*, a history of Flemish bobbin lace as it relates to the Catholic devotion to the Virgin Mary. Mother's passion for historical research and collecting continued until her passing in 1993. Her book was first published in chapters in *Lace Magazine International*, a quarterly magazine about laces, both old and new, of which I was the founding editor. Living in California at the time, I wrote nearly all the articles and was its Art Director, responsible for layout and print files for all 56 issues from 1986 to 2000. I made many lace friends over those 14 years.

The *Carriage of Lost Love* was inspired by nature with its endless variations in patterns in plants, rocks, clouds and animals. I have always enjoyed strings, knots and braids and became an avid crocheter when I was 15. I pored over books with Arabic geometric patterns and photos of snowflakes. I admired books by Ernest Haeckel such as *Art Forms in Nature*, *Radiolarians* and others. I was inspired by the innovative use of materials in the bobbin lace art of Kaethe Kliot.[2] Together with my mother I eventually met Kaethe in Berkeley, and we became friends. In her lace shop I discovered several books about contemporary Bohemian lace artists in the seventies, which I still admire.

I studied language and literature at the Jesuit University of Antwerp in 1969 to 1970. My language skills soon opened my heart to the wider world and that's how I met my husband, Burr Jerger. Burr witnessed the beginnings of my copper lace work, the first windows of the *Carriage of Lost Love*, and from that time on he impressed upon me that this creation was very important, that I had a duty to keep working at turning my vision into reality.

The project of the carriage began with just one panel, the Traveler window. It was a single-line drawing of a person's profile with wavy hair blowing in the wind, looking at a planet in space, all set in a field of Devonshire filling that I took straight from *The Book of Bobbin Lace Stitches* by Cook & Stott.[3] The drawing came together in less than a minute—a lucky fluke. I took it as a sign that I had to continue and work it out in wire. The Traveler was a magical 20" x 20" sheet of fire that sparked my imagination. She deserved a noble vehicle that would do justice to her beauty. Only then did I decide to build a ceremonial carriage, like the ones my mother had taken me to see at the Museo Dos Coches in Lisbon, Portugal, where she had to pull me out of the hall, because I could not bring myself to walk away. It was the summer of 1968.

In 1966, my younger brother Bruno, who was 15, offered to install extra lighting for me in my room. We lived in a historic nine-bedroom mansion built before WWI, big enough for a household of twelve. As his grateful apprentice, I saw him pull out of the wall the most amazing and brilliant copper wires and I am sure that is where I became enamored of the material.

On my first trip from California back to my family in Antwerp in 1977, mother was very happy when I asked her how to make bobbin lace. She showed me the basic stitches with sturdy linen thread using my godmother's hand-turned oak bobbins. These tools are nothing less than magic wands to me. The more I use them, the more they glisten. From my mother, I learned the basic rituals and stitches in a single two-hour session: winding bobbins, making knots for starting and ending threads, linen stitch, net stitch and how to make leaves. I returned to California with a large suitcase full of books, bobbins and rare Flemish linen threads. But upon my return, I wound grandma's magic wands with copper wire as soon as I could get my hands on some. I traded a large, white-cotton, crocheted "environment", a hanging sculpture, for my first one-pound spool of 30-gauge copper wire. I have never looked back. Copper lace is my medium of choice.

The most delicate bobbin laces of the *Spieghel Collection* are inherently women's work, and they express the emotions of a woman's life. They are anonymous works of art, bewitching under a magnifying glass. Joys, hopes, sorrows, grief--all of it is turned into ephemeral beauty by the continued work of the lacemaker's hands. The only real mistake we can make as a lacemaker is to quit, to give up on our dream.

I never thought of giving up, not even when wires kept breaking when I pulled them too tight. I developed my "wire touch" by doing. I have used clear-coated American Standard wire gauges, as heavy as gauge 10 and as fine as 38. Even heavy gauge copper wire must be handled gently and kinks are unforgiving, but the strength and brilliance of copper wire is what seduced me. It is even more enduring than linen. The perfectly round copper wire is manufactured to high scientific standards, and intended for generating, transmitting, and distributing electrical power. It makes the woven images shimmer in the light. Only with copper wire could I construct my *Carriage of Lost Love*. At first it seemed hard but eventually I mastered leaves and tallies. I invented wire grounds and braids that are not found in any books. The holes can be made much bigger in wire lace. The ground work progresses faster. Depending on how tight the weavers are pulled, the linen stitch can look either open and airy, or tight and solid. The rigidity of metal allows me to construct large sculptures. But my lace work does not come close to the virtuosity of the finest laces I have seen in the *Spieghel Collection.*

Per square inch, the eight windows of the *Carriage of Lost Love* have taken the longest time to create. After the Traveler was completed, I drew the pattern for the Trees window and worked it out with 30-gauge wire and simple net stitch, which emulated the bark of the real oak trees in the park near our childhood home. It took about two months from drawing to finished window. I was happy to have some 38-gauge wire for the smallest trees in the far distance. Both Trees windows are mounted in the center of the side

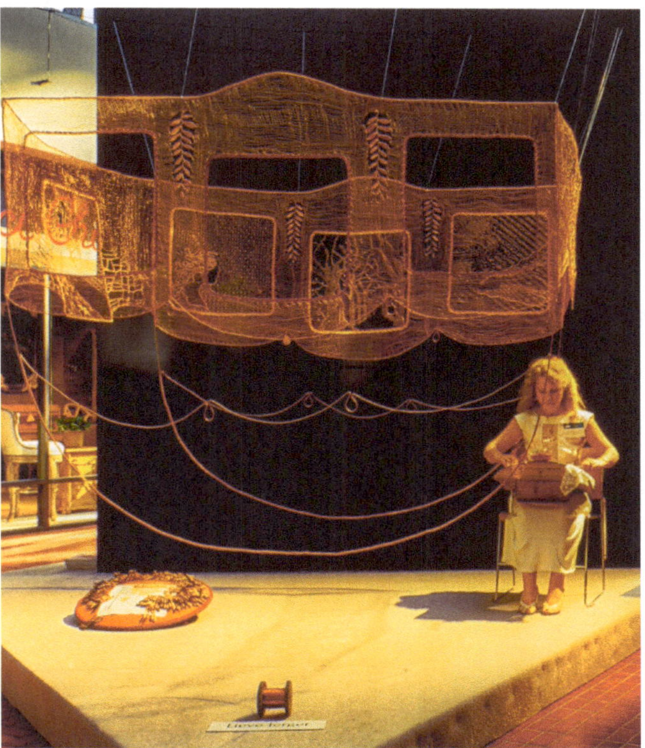

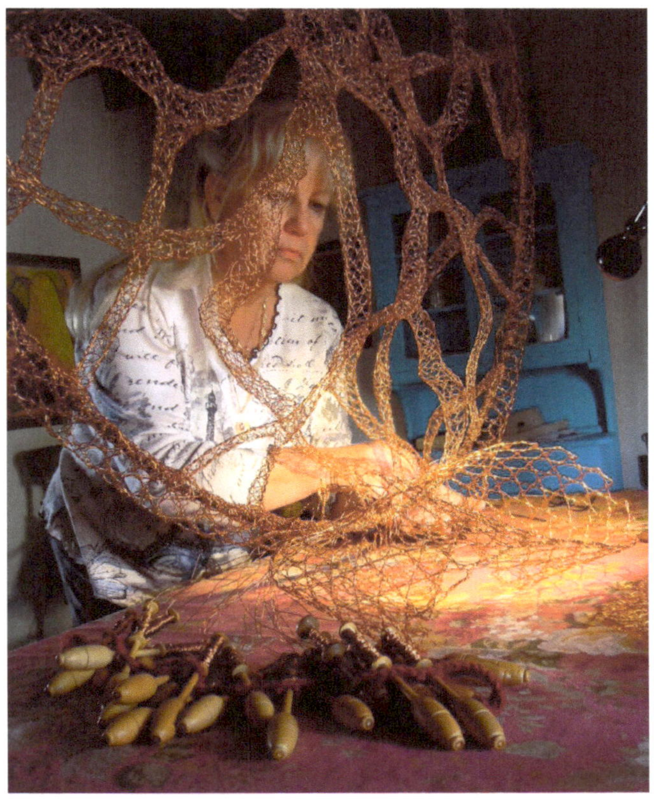

Lieve Jerger. *The Carriage of Lost Love.* Jerger working on the Carriage in 1985.

Lieve Jerger. *The Carriage of Lost Love.* Jerger working on the Carriage in 2007.

panels. On the opposite side I used the same tree pattern, but worked in the negative: all patches of sky and road are lace, but the trees were left open.

The Swan is a fellow traveler, seemingly adrift in a lake of teardrops. Coming to terms with my own sadness and turning the sad image into a joyful one took me six months of lacemaking. Like Penelope, I paused the work and re-drew the pattern for the ground nearly a hundred times. I erased more than I drew, constantly redesigning the reflections in the water until the sparkles made me happy. The park adjacent to our childhood home in Belgium has a castle and a lake with white swans. The Swan window is the third window on the left side panel of the Carriage.

The front window is a simple outline of the Traveler's right hand touching the screen, signaling the coachman to move ahead. The handprint is set into a panel of Arabic geometric inter-lacings, which first captivated me in the Alhambra in Granada. This window is worked in eight-strand linen stitch braids.

I gave the title *Pretending You Are Here* to the rear window with the lovers. It was completed in 1979. The Traveler's profile is riding backwards and facing the Lovers window in the rear. It is a sad goodbye, a physical absence deeply felt. This drawing took a few days and it felt so true to my mood that it helped me get over the loss of a friend and the loss of my brother Lucas. In *Pretending You Are Here*, I framed the figures embracing under an arch in a rock wall. The absent lover is rendered as negative space, firmly locked in the woman's embrace. Behind the ruins, a carriage is waiting. The stream of bright light coming through the arch becomes a waterfall. A vine climbs up the linen stitch stone wall of the ruins, and a small tree in net stitch has a support pole strapped to its trunk. A starry sky in virgin ground cascades above the scene. Stylized rocks and leafy plants are growing all around.

I designed the structural panels only after the first four windows were already completed. I admit that I was a little surprised myself when I saw how large the overall *Carriage of Lost Love* would become, but the realization filled me with anticipation for a lifetime of copper lace work.

The Butterfly window is still in progress: a daisy with a Fibonacci pattern in the seeds eludes me in the drawing. The Reflections window, most recently added, is a meditative collage of an open arched stone window in the Cistercian monastery in the California town of Vina, as it is reflected in a pool of water, with oak leaves drifting in from outside.

The lacemaking became more intense as I worked on the upper panels and later the wheels. Sometimes I didn't leave home for a week or more. I was still weaving wires in my dreams. Life took on a new dimension. Each window became a glowing icon in my own mind and took on more meaning as time went by. What started as a painful memory evolved into a source of healing and acceptance.

Long stretches of time passed by without any visible progress on the *Carriage of Lost Love*. I spent years doing office work, but I always visited the *Carriage* at dreamtime—before and after sleep—and like a best friend, she was always ready to give me courage and support. She needed me and I needed her.

In 1981 the former Army barracks in Angel's Gate Park were dedicated as a Cultural Center for the Arts in Los Angeles by then Mayor Tom Bradley. I was very fortunate to receive a two-room studio by the flagpole, which gave me the first opportunity to assemble the *Carriage* in progress and show it to visitors. At Angel's Gate Cultural Center, at UCLA Extension and at Coastline Community College, I taught copper lace classes to over 100 students. Many of them continued to work with copper wire and all of them remain cherished friends.

Angel's Gate also introduced me to many special people who became my friends for life: Honor Kirk, Joan Connor, Nick Kappes, Gordon Wagner, Joel Sansone, Harold Greene, Muriel and John Olguín, Paul Bouchard, Georgina Clarke, John Hylton, Louise Tasker, Loy Lewis, Susan Anderson, James Allen, Garr Kuhl, Spencer MacCallum, Emalie Caley, all my lace students, and many more.

After five years, the *Carriage* sculpture was disassembled and moved back to my home. Only in 2014 did I get another studio space to work in. This time it was an invitation from Spencer MacCallum and his wife Emalie in Viejo Casas Grandes, Chihuahua, Mexico. They offered me a residency at Casa Nopal, one of their gloriously restored old adobe homes, where I reassembled the *Carriage*, and where I constructed all four wheels of the *Carriage of Lost Love,* met other artists and made new friends.

The wheels were first imagined when I saw the up-ended root balls of fallen redwood trees in Northern California.

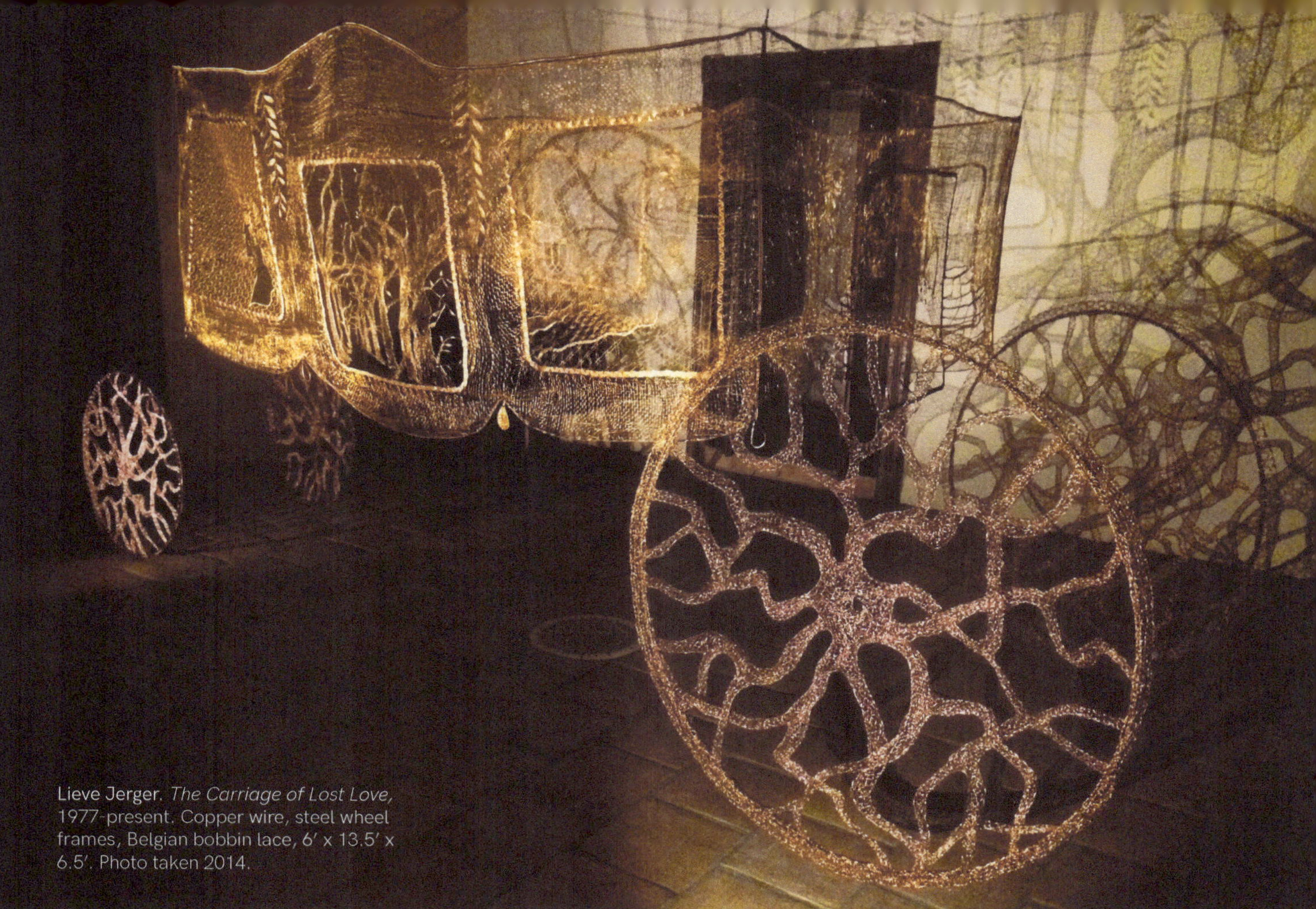

Lieve Jerger. *The Carriage of Lost Love,* 1977-present. Copper wire, steel wheel frames, Belgian bobbin lace, 6′ x 13.5′ x 6.5′. Photo taken 2014.

The large rear wheels measure 45" and are made in net stitch. I worked the pattern twice for each wheel, and two halves were sewn together to form three-dimensional branches. The large rear wheels were made with 23-gauge wire, and the smaller ones in the front were worked with 24-gauge wire. Technically, the wheels are an exploration into the third dimension. They have steel support rings inside. I calculated the exact wire gauge I would need to build the smaller front wheels from the scaled down pattern. I felt good about my otherwise poor numbers skills!

Although it is only legible in the imaginary tracks left on earth by the Carriage, I wrote this thought in mirror script around the big wheel tires: *lost-love-is-never-lost.* This healing wisdom is what the *Carriage of Lost Love* has been teaching me.

Artist Philip Dana Yeh, a lifelong friend of Burr Jerger and myself, wrote the fairytale *The Winged Tiger and the Lace Princess,*[4] in 1998, inspired by the *Carriage of Lost Love.* It is a love story for all ages about the importance of art, and with a Taoist ending. The book quickly sold out, hailed by all for its beautiful storyline and for Yeh's masterful watercolors. The first four windows of the large Carriage were superimposed digitally over the photos of a small copper lace model coach I had made just for this book.

Working on the *Carriage of Lost Love* has been a magical way for me to conquer sadness and subdue strong emotions. At times when language seems totally inadequate, a handwoven work of lace can reach deep into our hearts. It transcends every language. Lacemaking should never become a lost art.

As it is slowly nearing completion, the *Carriage of Lost Love* has taught me much about myself and about the meaning of life. My own perspective on the *Carriage* and the lessons I am learning are still very personal. I built my transparent vehicle in the first place for myself, but I hope that other people, whose heart and psyche are in distress, will find solace in seeing *The Carriage of Lost Love* and will take away from it the same wisdom it has taught me and kept me alive.

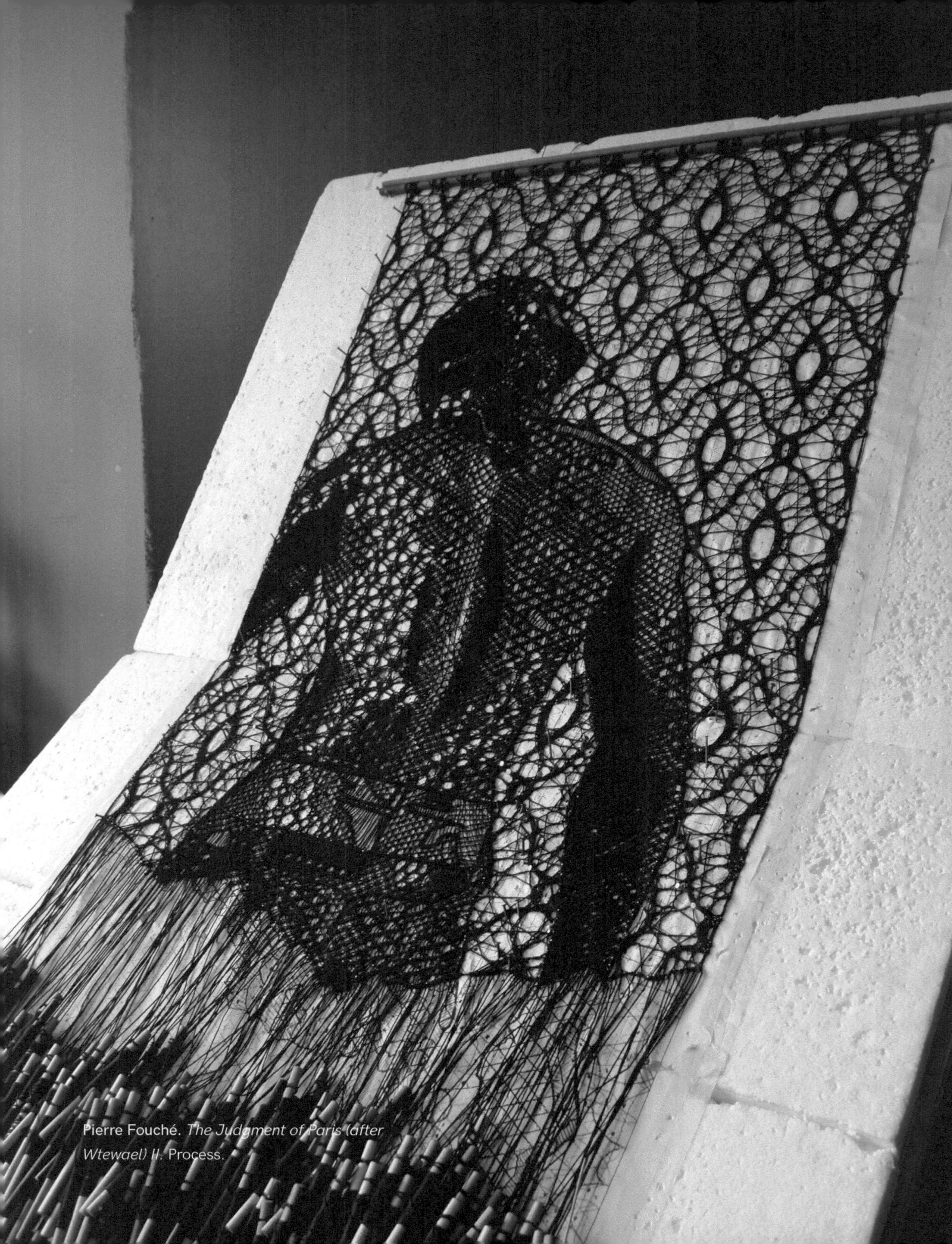

Pierre Fouché. *The Judgment of Paris (after Wtewael) II*. Process.

# The Artists

Manca Ahlin
Jane Atkinson
Daniela Banatova
Dagmar Beckel-Machyckova
J Carpenter
Choi+Shine
Jill Nordfors Clark
Milča Eremiášová
Pierre Fouché
Laura Friesel
Alex Goldberg
Maggie Hensel-Brown
Ágnes Herczeg
Ros Hills
Veronika Irvine
Lieve Jerger
Nava Lubelski
Dorie Millerson
Penny Nickels
Wako Ono
E.J.Parkes
Lenka Suchanek
Lauran Sundin
Olivia Valentine
Nicole Valsesia-Lair
Denise Watts
Louise West
Ashley Williams

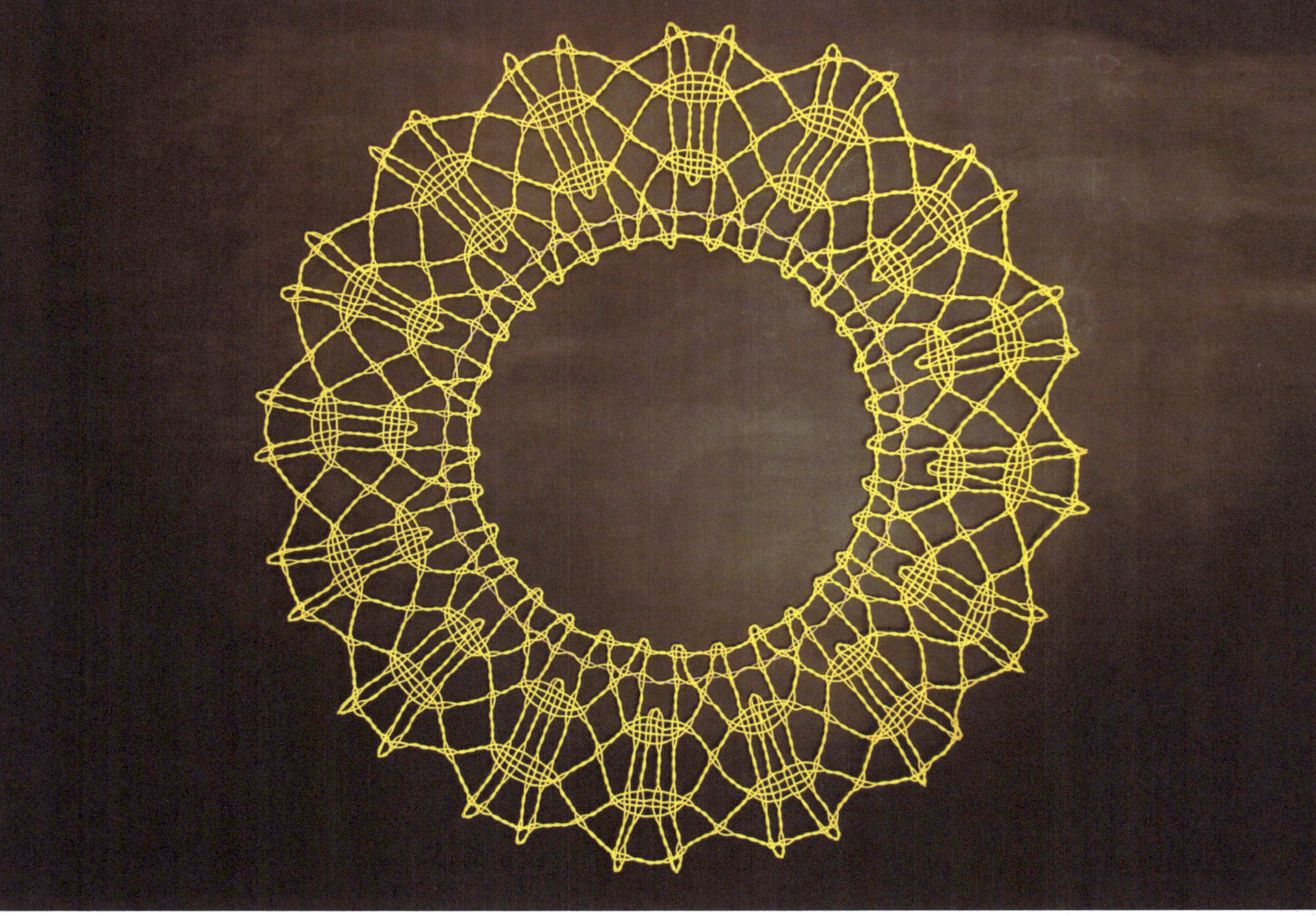

## Manca Ahlin

Manca Ahlin grew up in the highlands of Western Slovenia in the town of Žiri where, in her estimate, nearly half of the population knows how to make bobbin lace.[5] Ahlin attended the Lace School in Žiri, which has been in operation for 112 years and is one of the major centers of lacemaking in the region. In Žiri, the lace school operates almost like a day-care facility filling in the gaps of time that fall between formal school day and the work schedules of the parents, both in the morning and the evening. Ahlin describes her lace teacher as a great storyteller who would even help with homework. The lace school students would travel around the country doing lacemaking demonstrations at tourist events and participating in lace festivals where Ahlin was a frequent award winner. While still in primary school Ahlin began to draw lace patterns that were popular enough that she was soon selling them at these events.

As an adult, Ahlin studied production design and architecture in Ljubljana and Barcelona, directing her focus towards contemporary, computer driven methods of design. Besides architectural design, she created virtual environments for a number of architectural offices, private clients and museums, among them the Virtual Museum of Ljubljana. After years of successful and award-winning collaborations in architecture, Ahlin became increasingly interested in the connection between architectural space and lace — its appearance and structure, material and decorative possibilities. Her latest works in spatial lace installation have received international acclaim, with illustrations published worldwide. Currently based in New York, Ahlin explores the intersection between traditional craft and contemporary design through her brand Mantzalin. She moves easily through several layers of scale in her fabrications, from jewelry pieces to large architectural installations.

Ahlin describes her transition from the world of virtual environments to that of direct contact with materials as one of reaching back to her origins. Although very contemporary, her large installations owe a debt to the style of lace that was practiced in Žiri and nearby Idrija. Slovenian lacemakers

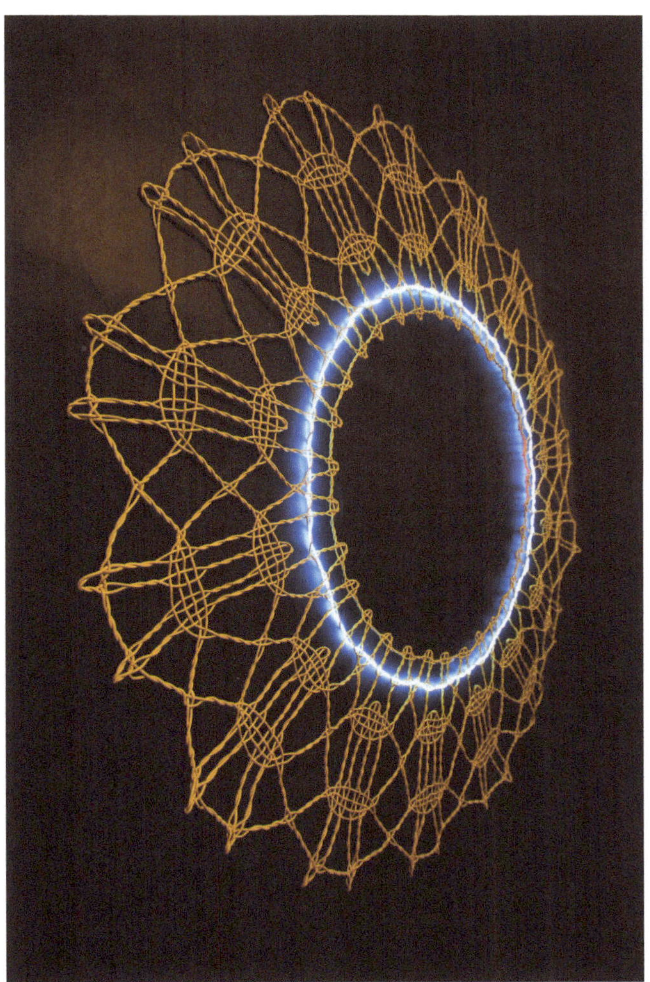

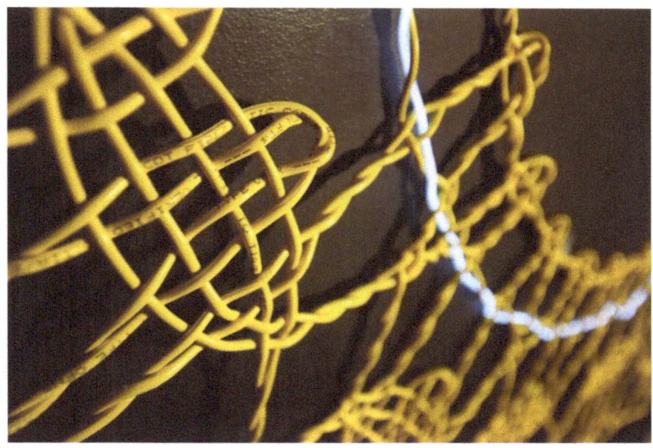

typically work in a tape lace style with a small number of bobbins. They use a simple bolster pillow held in a basket. The worker can reposition the bolster within the basket so that the working area is always optimally exposed. The bobbins are suspended in air and worked in the hand as are most Eastern European laces. In Ahlin's large scale work she does not use a bolster, but instead works the lace pattern on the floor physically following the route of the tape.

Manca Ahlin. *Corona*, 2014. Fiber Optic Cable, EL wire. 5′ x 5′. Photo: Manca Ahlin.

Manca Ahlin. *Corona*. Illuminated.

Manca Ahlin. *Corona*. Detail.

Manca Ahlin. *Corona*. Process.

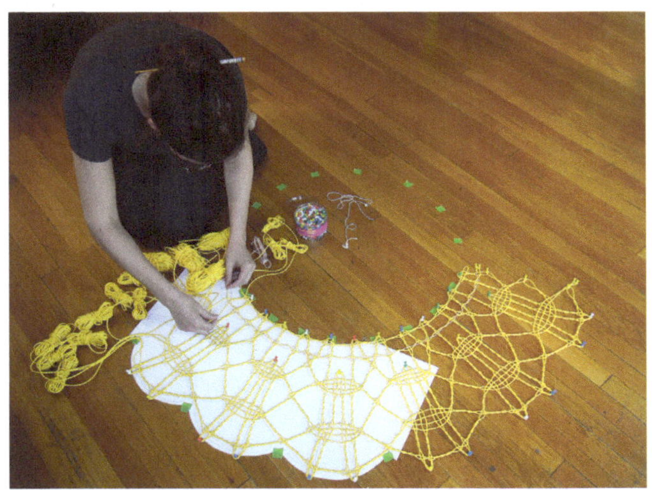

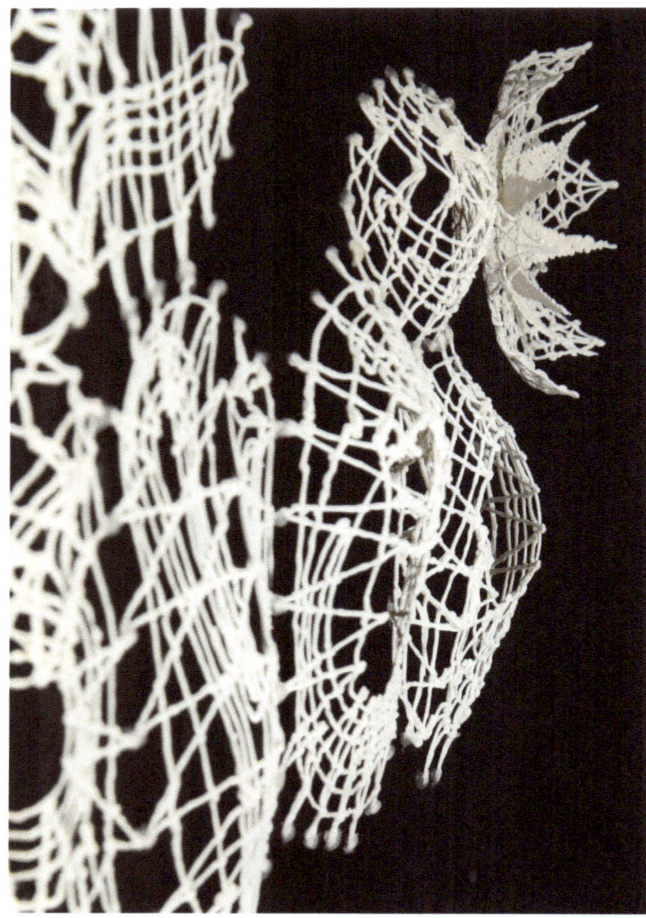

## Artist Statement

As a trained architect I am used to thinking about an object through its relationship to space. Lace has traditionally been made and used as a flat piece of fabric, either as interior decoration or in fashion. I want to subvert this constraint and make lace again a relevant player in the field of contemporary design, to discard its stigma of a benign little doily on grandmother's shelf. Computer-aided design methods allow me to create shapes previously impossible to conceive by hand. Through the change in scale and use of construction materials and tools I add to the traditional two-dimensional lace structures a third, spatial dimension and expand its scope of functional uses.

## Corona

The Solar Corona is the extended outer layer of the Sun's atmosphere. It extends millions of kilometers into space and has a temperature of approximately two million kelvins, yet it is 10 billion times less dense than the atmosphere of the Earth at sea level. The corona is a million times less bright than the inner part of the sun, and thus we can only see it during a solar eclipse. From my experience of working in architecture, I have realized how we tend to neglect the natural environment, how much of the potential and resources in nature we just don't take advantage of, perhaps just by the correct orientation of the building, the use of insulation and other sustainable materials or the collection of solar energy. Yet some still cite the sun as the reason for climate change instead of admitting that it is our consumerist society that is to blame.

With *Corona*, I want to transgress the scale and materiality of the traditional lace doily: blown up about ten times, it surpasses its use as a shelf decoration to become an independent object in space which is made of reused fiber-optic cable instead of delicate silk thread. One of the central cables is replaced with electroluminescent wire that emits light—like the photosphere layer of the Sun.

## Mani Lace Wall

Trekking through the Himalayan landscapes and villages (in the region under the influence of Tibetan Buddhism), we passed by numerous Buddhist structures. Prayer flags, prayer wheels and mani stones alike were all mostly inscribed with the mantra 'Om Mani Padme Hum'. Visually, their graphical aspect struck me with its resemblance to lace structures. On a basic level, not unlike repetitively chanting the mantra while meditating, lacemaking with its repetitive movements creates similar effect of relaxation, connection and peace of mind. The sound of OM (AUM) is said to vibrate on the same frequency as everything throughout the nature. It connects us to all other living beings. *The Mani Lace Wall* is representing this connection between Us, Nature, and the Universe.

Mani Stones piled-up into a prayer wall, are made in different shapes, designs, and stone materials. Inspired by them, my Mani Lace Wall is assembled of various lace pieces - also in different shapes, designs, and rope materials.

Manca Ahlin. *Mani Lace Wall,* 2018. Scale Model
Photo: Manca Ahlin.

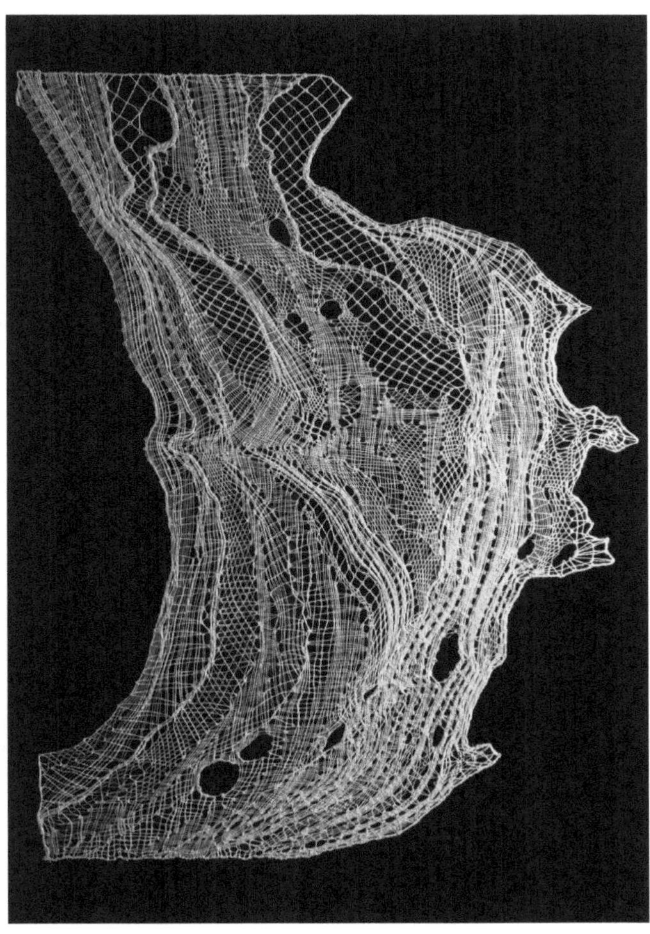

## Jane Atkinson

Hugely influential in the world of contemporary lace, Jane Atkinson has moved from strength to strength since the 1970s along a path she has created between traditional bobbin lace and contemporary craft.

Atkinson is a fourth generation lacemaker. Her great-grandmother, grandmother, mother and aunts learned lacemaking in the 1920s at classes given by the Women's Institute.[6] Although she was exposed to lacemaking in her family, Atkinson did not learn the skill from them. The lack of learning opportunities in the early 1970s resulted in Atkinson being largely self-taught in bobbin lacemaking. She says that her first introduction to bobbin lace prompted a "visceral reaction. I felt I saw stars. I knew this was for me…This was like being handed an intriguing board game without the rule book."

Atkinson's book *Pattern Design for Torchon Lace* [7] was a significant milestone in late 20th century lace. Historically, the people who designed the lace were designers, mostly men. The people who made the lace were lacemakers, mostly women. As lacemaking transitioned from a commercial activity into a hobby, old ways continued to prevail, with the lacemakers never entering the realm of lace design. Atkinson's book was among the first to give instructions, and permission, to lacemakers to design their own pieces.

Although interested in more complex laces, Atkinson realized that a book about design should be oriented toward the simplest of laces, and the lace that most people knew how to make, namely Torchon-- a geometric lace made on a 90-degree grid. To her surprise she found that Torchon offered an extremely wide scope for design. Exploiting opportunities to experiment with scale, working on deformed grids, and including unusual threads all contributed to a more contemporary design aesthetic.

Her second book, *Contemporary Lace for You*[8], expanded on these themes incorporating logarithmic grids and complicated color manipulation.

Atkinson describes her preference for continuous lace[9] over part lace in this way:

*The threads flow through the work from one end to the other. They might deviate into weaving as a worker pair, and dance around in complex sets of crossings and twistings for special stitches, but the threads find their way through this maze to cross the finishing line together;*

A class with a Czech lace teacher in which she learned the Czech method of working with relatively few bobbins, weaving tapes of various widths and pushing in pins without reference to an underlying grid proved intriguing. Atkinson recognized that the Czech form of lacemaking, not relentlessly tied to a grid, is better suited to the abstract, organic shapes in her landscape.

When she began *Seableed* she thought that its striated structure could best be interpreted in Czech-style tapes, joined successively. However, she found out that the piece

Jane Atkinson. *Seableed,* 2018. Bobbin lace, 23″ x 17″. Photo: Peter Smith.

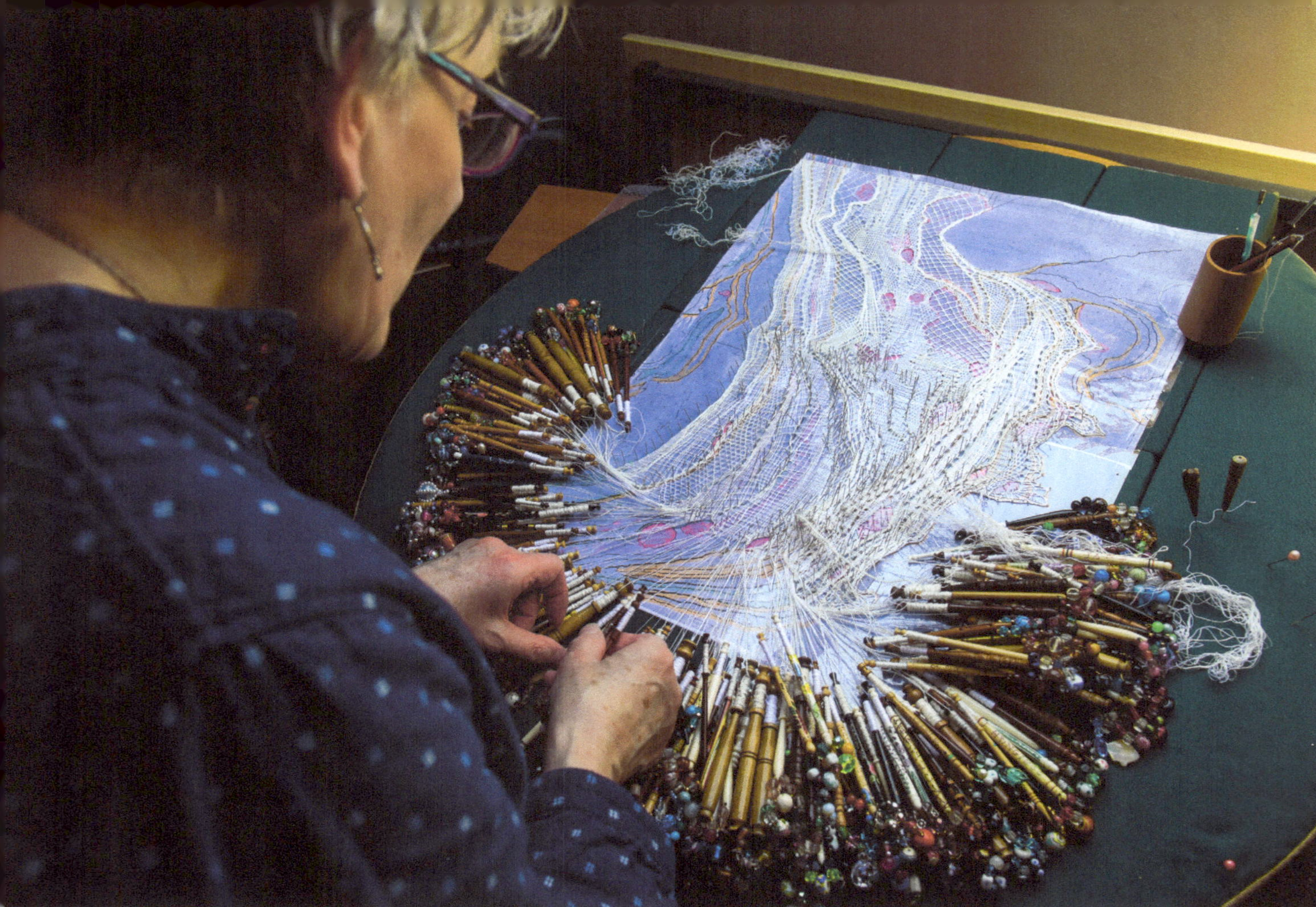

Jane Atkinson. *Seableed.* Process. Photo: Elementum Journal.

was too complicated for that, and decided to make the tapes simultaneously, weaving threads from one area to the next, returning to the principles of continuous lace while achieving the aesthetic of tape lace.

*Seableed* is the first in a new series of pieces about the marsh, a topic she has already explored in her distinctive contemporary torchon style in *Oxygen*, a series of four panels about climate change which will be on display in a show of Atkinson's work called *Ebb'n'Flow.*[10] In *Seableed* which was created for *Lace, not Lace*, she developed a hybrid method of working, using the grid when she wanted to, but using Czech tape lace techniques such as adding and subtracting threads of different characteristics and subverting stitches to create new textures.

Fifteen different threads, all linen, but differently spun, and of different thicknesses are present in *Seableed*. They move through the work in subtle and unexpected ways sometimes creating the appearance of streaks when placed next to thinner threads, other times moving surreptitiously through an otherwise even cloth stitch. In some places passive threads are packed together in cloth stitch to create a solidly white area. Half stitch areas present a medium tone. Dark pockets of water are achieved with the use of variations of simple torchon ground creating negative space. Atkinson relies on the simplest of stitches, half stitch, cloth stitch and whole stitch, and does not employ sophisticated grounds. The use of "jeden", a Czech technique in which it is possible to position the passives exactly in place by twisting the worker pair, is used to create the sinuous curves of the oozing organic material.

In *Seableed*, Atkinson has in her words "really tried to push the boat out, to test myself and learn new things." She has departed from her comfort zone technically, to create a sophisticated lace work that ruminates on our fragile environment and the impact of climate change.

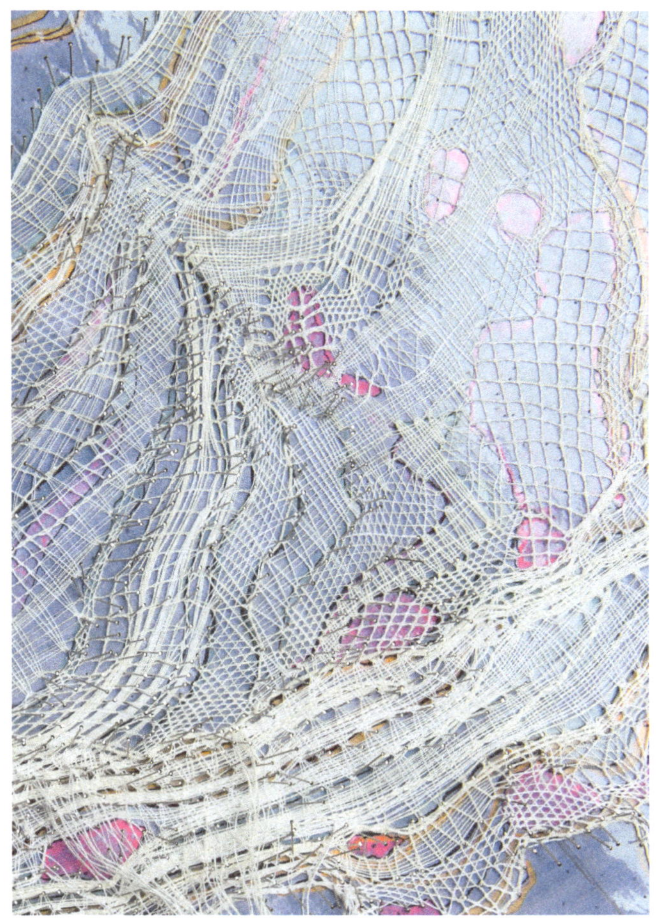

I lift inspiration from my local landscape for contemporary lace, to create conversation pieces about our changing climate. My daily walk, since 2000, around Stanpit Marsh in Christchurch Harbour, Dorset, UK, has led me to chart the way global change is affecting local phenomena.

It can be hard to understand the way high levels of carbon dioxide in industrial emissions have been absorbed globally by the sea, warming it. This can lead to stronger hurricanes in the Caribbean, or higher river temperatures in the UK, all of which can upset delicate ecology. For example, fish such as salmon breed only at certain temperatures, but not if it is too warm; healthy river systems have evolved with indigenous plants, but can be upset by alien invaders enabled by climate change.

Christchurch lies at the mouth of the Hampshire river Avon, part of a system of chalk streams and rivers famous the world over for their fly fishing for trout and salmon. The Pacific red seaweed *Gracilaria vermiculophylla* arrived there in 2017, brought in on craft visiting from neighboring Poole Harbour, its first sighting in Dorset. When it rotted in the autumn, stinking fumes enveloped the locality; seaweed that rots in the water also acidifies it, warming it further.

*Seableed* derives from spectacular ribbons of viscosity that seeped out from a clump of rotting seaweed, pulled by the wind into looping festoons that covered the surface of a pool in saltmarsh at the harbor's edge. It is the first of a series that will record the beauty and recall the misery.

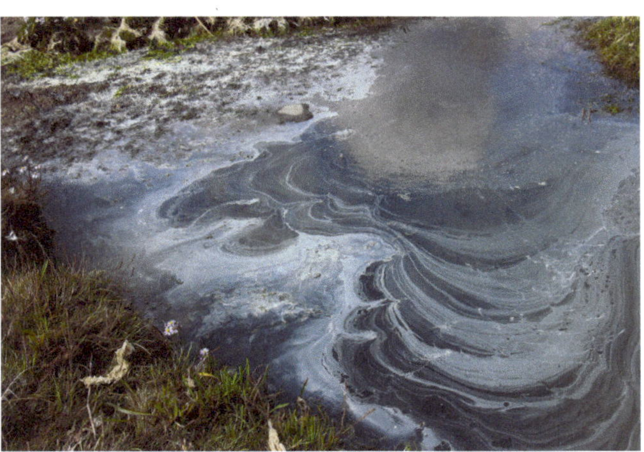

Jane Atkinson. *Seableed.* Detail. Photo: Elementum Journal.

Rotting seaweed in Stanpit Marsh, the artist's inspiration. Photo: Jane Atkinson.

## Daniela Banatova

Born in Ostrava, Czechoslovakia, Daniela Banatova studied fabric design, specializing in bobbin lace at the School of Art Design. At Masaryk University, in Brno she earned a master's degree in art history and aesthetics. After teaching art in several venues in Czech Republic she moved to Belleview, Florida where she takes an active role in the artistic community. She often exhibits her work and is the co-founder of an arts institution called Spirit of the International Art.[11]

Banatova's process begins with making an actual size drawing on a large piece of paper and pinning it to the lace pillow. Rather than working out her intricate color schemes beforehand, she likes to create freely on the pillow, like a painter, choosing and combining colors extemporaneously. First, she creates the strong outlines with a crochet thread in dense cloth stitch. Different weights of thread can be used for the filling. When she wants a part of the composition to be "poetic light" she uses fine sewing thread.[12]

In *Danae*, Banatova engages in sophisticated color play by using different colors for the worker pairs than for the passive pairs in the cloth stitch. When the passives and worker pairs are equally spaced, the colors blend. When the passives are tightly packed, their color predominates. Fillings in black assume different tones, the lightest being rendered in point ground and in fine thread. Contrary to the usually regular appearance of point ground which is often controlled by pins and regulated by graph paper, Banatova has allowed the point ground in her composition to assume an organic appearance. Long, twisted sewings, a hallmark of contemporary Czech lace, join areas while creating the appearance of voids.

It is very exciting for me to combine the shapes, colors and matrix of textile to create visual abstract patterns. Almost all of my works are inspired by nature, but expressed primarily in abstraction

Organic forms of my designs exude primordial essence. I would like my technique to be [a] matrix of cells coming together to create a new form of life. I strive for my composition to be a balanced harmony of positive and negative space, texture and colors.[13]

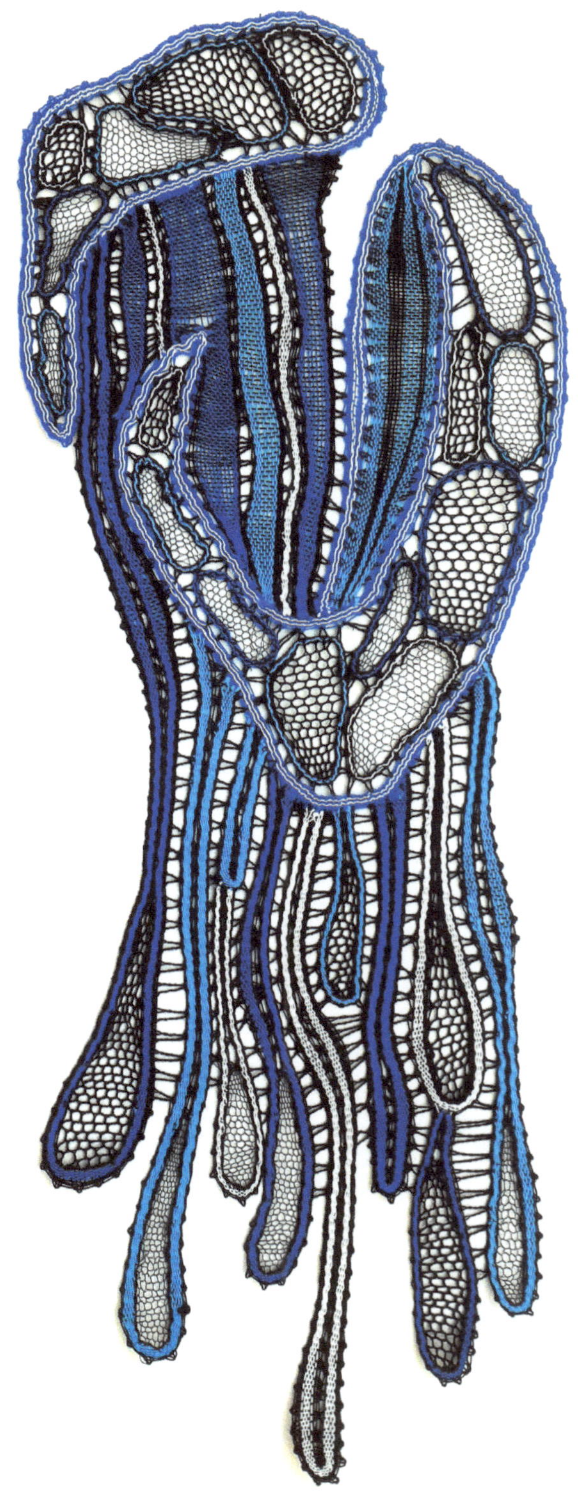

Daniela Banatova. *Danae*, 2014. Bobbin lace, 40" x 20". Photo: Daniela Banatova.

## Dagmar Beckel-Machyckova

Born in Prague, Czechoslovakia, Dagmar Beckel-Machyckova became so fascinated with bobbin lace that she took a degree in the subject at the Institute of Art Manufacturing in Prague, winning 2nd place in a country wide Young Lacemaker's Design Competition. She was fortunate to be able to study with Milča Eremiášová, one of the foremost lace artists of the 20th century. Beckel-Machyckova moved to the United States in 2001 to pursue her master's degree in Business Administration and Communication, and now owns and manages, with her husband, a high-tech business that specializes in services to improve neo-natal calf care in the dairy industry. This focus has manifested itself in her philosophical interest in food production which is explored in her work *Habitats of Hypocrisy.*

After years of subordinating her artistic work to her business, Beckel-Machyckova has been able to return to bobbin lace, writing articles for several lace magazines and becoming a popular teacher specializing in Czech lace. Due to the political disruptions of the last century, Czech modern lace has not been widely practiced in the United States. Beckel-Machyckova's classes have been enthusiastically received by lacemakers who are eager to creatively interpret drawings in the Czech lace style.

Although Beckel-Machckova's work is less ornate, and more minimalist, the influence of her mentor Eremiášová is evident in her use of perspective, and in the precisely located worker pairs that are characteristic of Czech lace and are frequently drawn on the pattern before work rather than developing organically from the interaction of thread and stitch. Rather than working strictly in two dimensions, Beckel-Machyckova has placed the habitats, both the houses, and the animal hutches, at a distance from the background to emphasize the way that food animals' housing is a reflection of the human environment.

Over population and urbanization has separated most consumers from their food. With less than 1% of the US population farming, consumers have lost their relationship to how food is grown and are forced to rely on often misleading advertisements. Fast food chains regularly over-promise and use marketing gimmicks to charge for premium product, while only serving the regulatory standard.

Food processors often claim free-range animal product and then add fine print to explain that it really isn't so. Yet the consumer, so disconnected from the actual farmer, has little ability to discern what is and isn't true.

*Habitats of Hypocrisy* shows rows of houses above rows of calf hutches thus positioning a mirror to today's society and our ability to provide food for ourselves, depicting that the way we take care of our animals is a clear reflection of the way we live. As the population grows, our cities have essentially become concentrated people feeding operations, demanding large volumes of food on a daily basis. The challenge of feeding so many people in a cost efficient and timely manner naturally leads to the creation of concentrated animal feeding operations in order to satisfy the demand. Yet these operations have come under much criticism precisely from the urbanites who cause their existence.

I invite the viewer to reflect on how humans shape the world around them and what can be done for long-term sustainability.

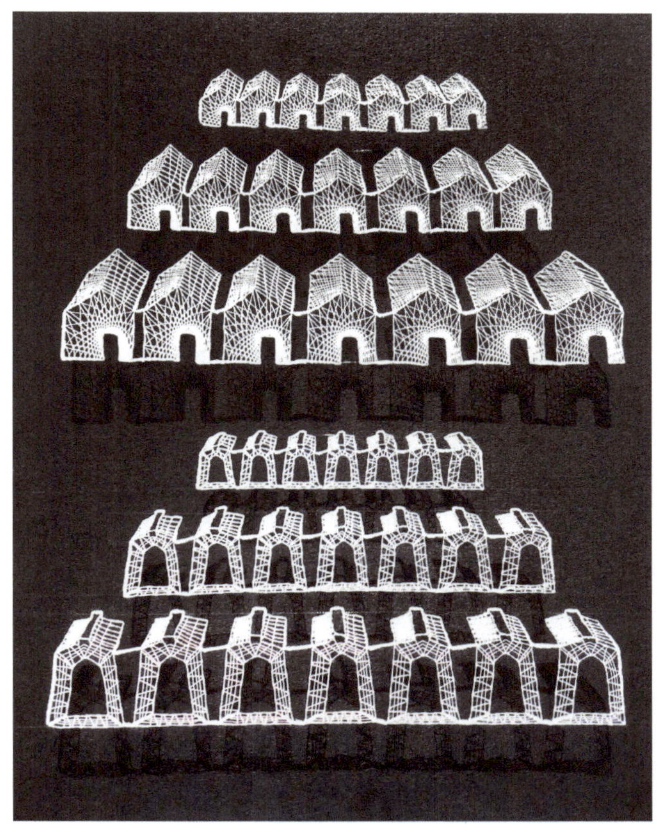

Dagmar Beckel-Machyckova. *Habitats of Hypocrisy*, 2018. Bobbin lace, cotton, 24″ x 18″. Photo: Dagmar Beckel-Machyckova.

## J Carpenter

J Carpenter was first exposed to lacemaking in the pages of novels that she read when she was young. In these novels lacemaking was described as a difficult, painful form of labor, often the only recourse for poverty-stricken women and those whom social conditions had rendered "unmarriable". Carpenter became fascinated with the socio-political history of lacemaking, the hardship of the lives of lacemakers, the damaging effects of lacemaking on health and sight, that resulted in a product that was so exquisite in detail that it can barely be appreciated without the use of a microscope.

Carpenter earned a BA in Visual Arts from Rutgers University where she was trained in painting. When she first became interested in lace she created a lace like effect by embroidering over the paintings, transitioning to embroidery that looked like lace, and finally learning to make lace. She joined the Lost Art Lacers of North Jersey where she received bobbin lace instruction from Pat Morris and moral support from the other members.

In time she began to create lace sculptures including a series of houses. In these pieces Carpenter explores her own desire to create a safe and happy home life, seeking marriage or security in romantic relationships. She feels that she and her age mates are working endlessly, purposelessly, trying to create a sense of security that is only an illusion. Drawing both joy and pain from labor, she finds lace to be a perfect symbol for this dichotomy. Lace is beautiful, terribly time intensive to create, and results in a pleasing, although rather useless finished product.

The word "citrinitas" is a term used in alchemy, the phase of the process of fiery purification in which an object physically becomes gold. This union with fire, called alchemical marriage, leads to a rebirth in the destruction of the original substance. Carpenter relates this transmutation to a process of personal growth in which her preconceptions of what constitutes a conventional happy life have been burned to achieve the spiritual and emotional cleansing necessary to create a better life.

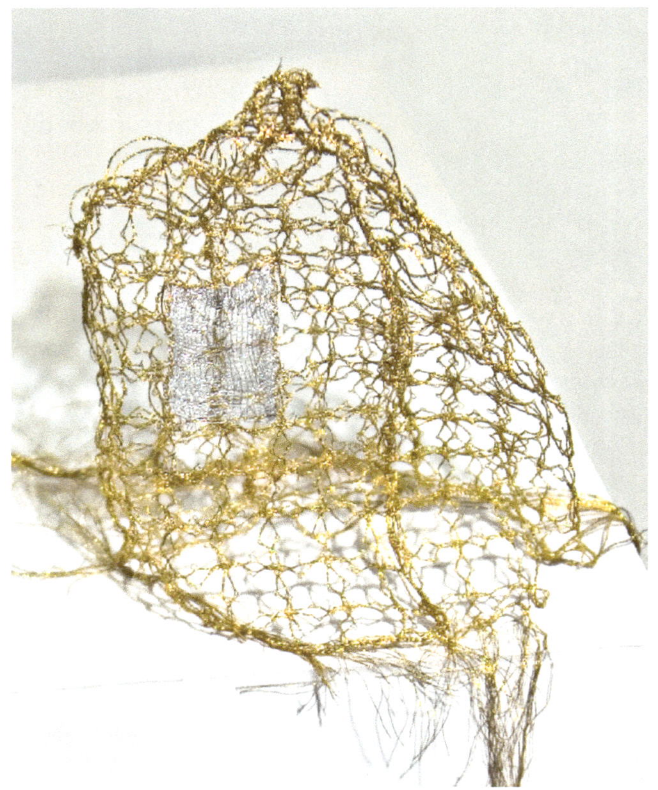

I am interested in how the grueling process of lace making and needlework relates to their purely decorative finished products and how this relationship is emblematic of much familial, social, and cultural effort. Just as lace garments neither shield nor warm their wearers, our domestic and cultural institutions often fall short in their promises of sanctuary, safety, and social justice. And yet, just as with lacemaking, the impulse to always do more persists, an impulse rooted in and nourished by hope.

The images that I portray reconstruct the paradox implicit in this hope. The seeming quixotic absurdity of the exhaustive effort it requires contrasts with its intrinsic personal, professional, and aesthetic rewards. Though a house arduously constructed of lace cannot provide physical sanctuary with its permeable thresholds drawing into confusion the very notion of interiority vs. exteriority itself and of who is being protected from what, these structures, distilled from their promises, endure as delicate images of the labor and aspirations from which they were constructed.

J Carpenter. *Citrinitas*, 2012. Handmade lace, 36″, width and depth vary by installation.

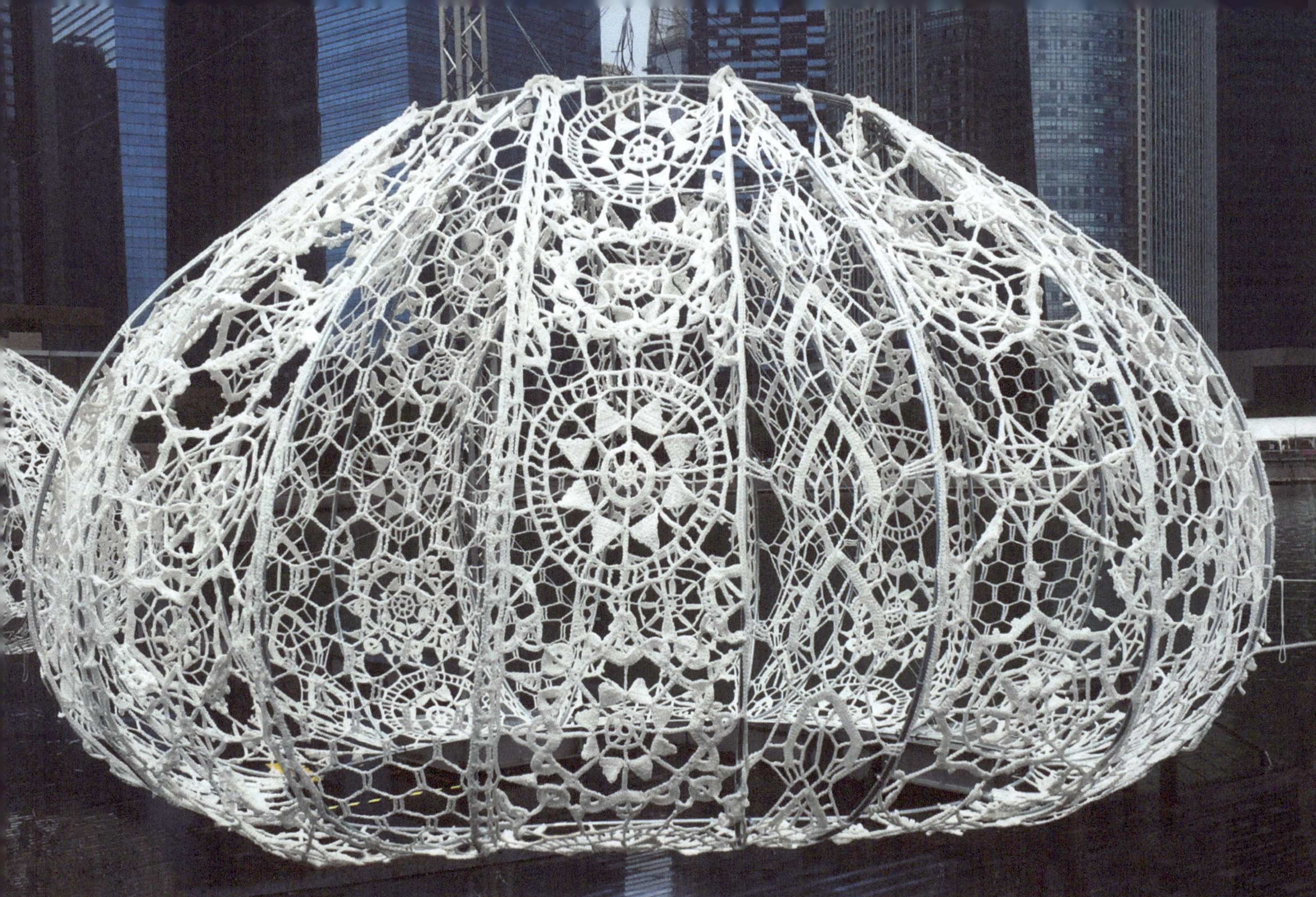

## Choi + Shine

Boston based design firm Choi+Shine first garnered the attention of the lace world with a piece called *The Lace*, a super-sized Dutch cap which hovered over the Herengracht canal in Amsterdam as part of the 2016 Amsterdam Light Festival.[14] Jin Choi referred to a book of historical reticella patterns published in 1890 by the thread company Dollfus-Mieg and authored by Thérèse de Dillmont.[15] *Reticella* is a geometric needle lace popular in the late 16th and early 17th centuries. She quickly realized that constructing the patterns in needle lace would be unworkable due to the size of the pieces and the lack of workers who knew how to make needle lace. She opted to translate them into crochet, another lace technique with origins in the 19th century which gives the appearance of needle lace but works up more quickly. With the adoption of a more widely practiced technique Choi+Shine was able to complete the work using volunteer artisans.

*The Lace* was followed by *The Urchins*, made for the 2017 Marina Bay Ilight Festival held in Singapore. *The Urchins* required 50 volunteers to crochet, many drawn from the lace community. Most people who know how to make lace already know how to crochet, since that is a common progression in skill acquisition. This is the first time *The Urchins* have been displayed in the United States.

This project is inspired by sea urchin shells, which are enclosed yet lightweight, delicate, and open. Their textured and permeable surface interacts with light and creates openness, while the pattern's mathematical repetition brings visual rhythm and harmony. The project mimics this orderly, repetitive pattern and soft forms, achieving a visual harmony from the contrast between nature and the man-made environment and aims to create a sense of place with an intricate, calm and simple object.

Choi + Shine Architects. *The Urchins*, 2017. Galvanized metal, nylon, polypropylene and marine grade cords. Three pieces each 8.85′ tall and 16.4′ in diameter. Photo: The Urchins © 2017 Choi + Shine Architects.

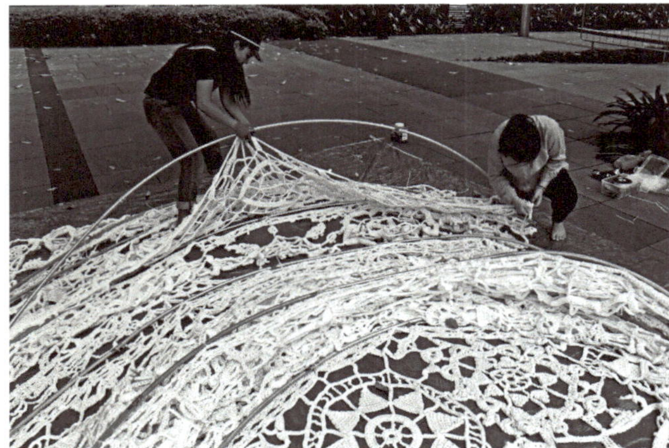

The lace symbolically weaves different people and cultures, while physically, the openings in the surface create patterns of light against the sky, water and town, a juxtaposition of a permeable surface on different visual layers

*The Urchins* were designed to interact with natural light during the day, and glow when illuminated at night. When viewers enter into *the Urchins*, they will be surrounded by a single layer of glowing, lacy surface, where they can enjoy the detail and texture of *the Urchins* and see the sky, the water and scenic Clinton through this visual filter. When other viewers see the occupants in *the Urchins*, the occupants will glow with the lacy room, creating an illusion of ethereal levitation of the occupants, while the occupants become a part of the work.

*The Urchins* also respond to the wind and touch of the viewers: *the Urchins* and their shadows rotate or move slowly as if they are pendulums. The rhythmic and repetitive movement of the Urchins creates a sense of time and contributes to the tranquil nature of the sculpture.

Generally, lace is small in scale, and often private. Seeing the mysteriously hovering and glowing large lacy objects in a public space causes the viewers to stop and gaze. This momentary pause of the mundane routine of our life would hopefully give us an opportunity to find the poetry around us.

Choi + Shine Architects. *The Urchins.* Attaching the crochet to the supporting structure. Photo: The Urchins © 2017 Choi + Shine Architects.

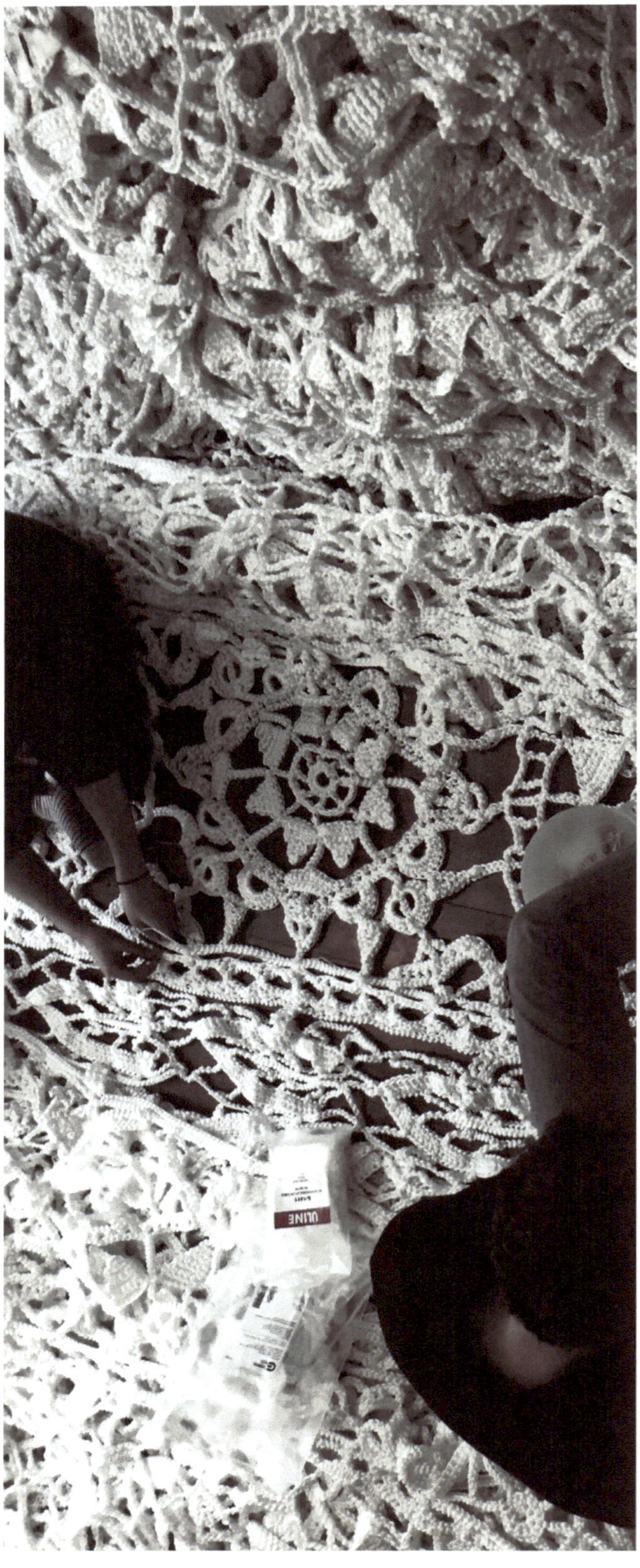

Choi + Shine Architects. *The Urchins.* Assembling the pieces. Photo: The Urchins © 2017 Choi + Shine Architects.

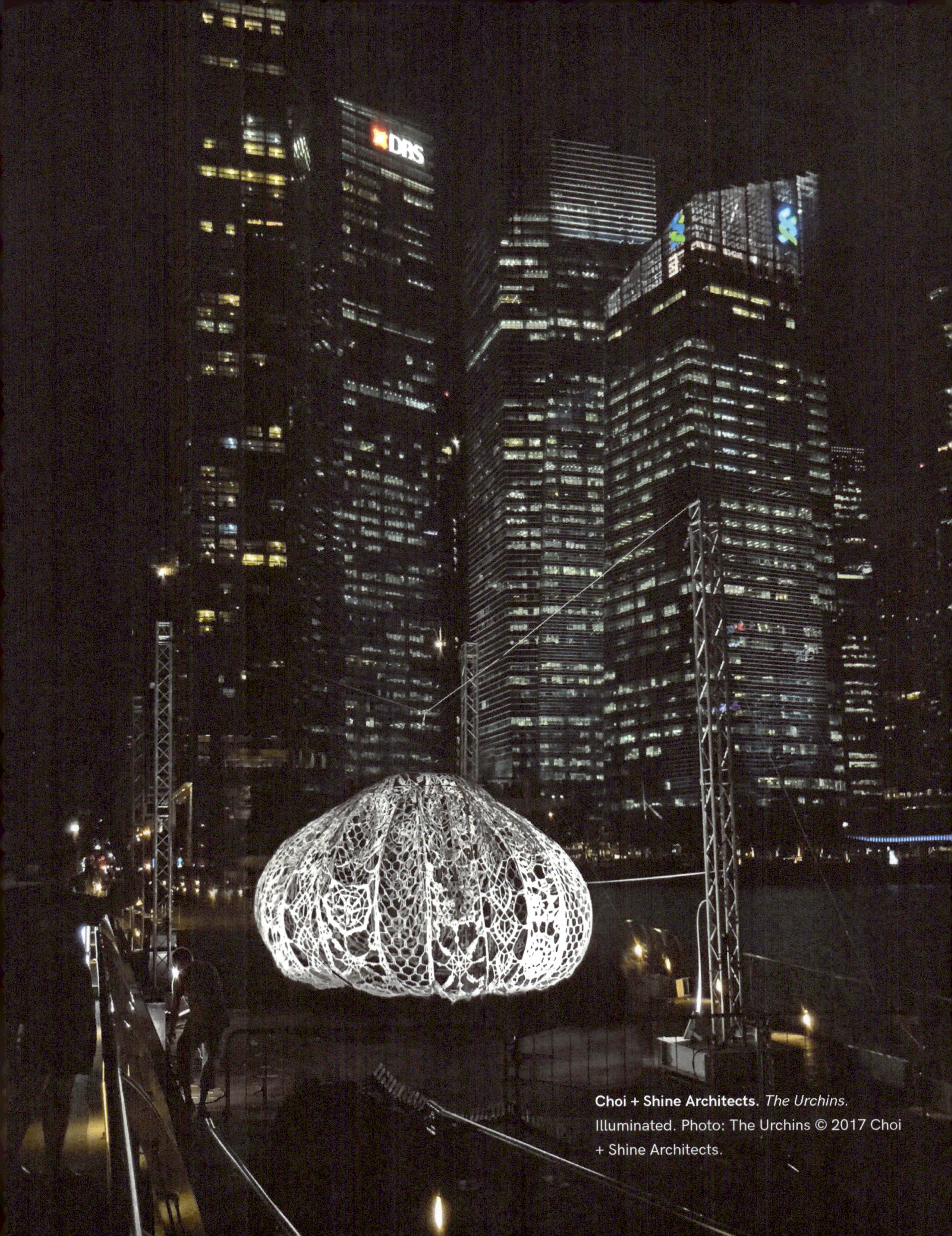


**Choi + Shine Architects.** *The Urchins.* Illuminated. Photo: The Urchins © 2017 Choi + Shine Architects.

## Jill Nordfors Clark

Jill Nordfors Clark occupies a unique niche in the world of needle lace. Her book *Needle Lace and Needleweaving: A New Look at Traditional Stitches*[16] was published in 1974, one of the first books of the needle lace revival and an eye-opening inspiration for many who became needle lacemakers. However, for the last 20 years, Clark is better known for working needle lace with hog gut, better known as sausage casing, which can be bought in butcher stores. Pliable when wet, the gut takes dye well and hardens into rigidity when dry, enabling needle lace to become sculpture. Her work with gut was inspired by the work of Native Americans of the Pacific Northwest who historically worked with seal and walrus gut to make clothing and vessels. Clark is a beachcomber and collector of natural found objects which she incorporates into her stitched gut lace, expressing a fresh West Coast aesthetic. [17]

Clark claims that she learned to make needle lace by accident. As an embroiderer in the early 1970s she met author and embroiderer Jacqueline Enthoven who suggested that there should be a book on needle lace and that Clark should write it for Enthoven's publisher. Since none of Clark's contemporaries knew what needle lace was, she had to learn from actual samples and from books largely dating from the 1880s. Clark studied the *Encyclopedia of Needlework*[18] by Thérèse de Dillmont, the *Encyclopedia of Victorian Needlework*[19] by Saward and Caulfeild which were being reprinted in this era, as well as the *Anchor Manual of Needlework*[20], a compendium of instructional manuals copyrighted by J and P Coats, the thread company.

As a result of her book emerging on the embroidery scene Clark was asked to teach needle lace workshops throughout the US, in the UK, and in New Zealand. During this time she met other members of the contemporary needle lace community such as Jan Beaney, Jean Littlejohn, Ros Hills, Constance Howard and Barbara Lee Smith, all of whom became her friends.

In 1999 Clark issued a second book *Needle Lace: Techniques and Inspiration*[21] which included revised and additional stitches and instructions on the use of gut. Since the use of gut requires a trip to a butcher shop followed by a multi-step rinsing process and time critical molding operation, the detailed instructions accompanied by 9 photographs of the process is a very useful addition to the canon of needle lace techniques.[22]

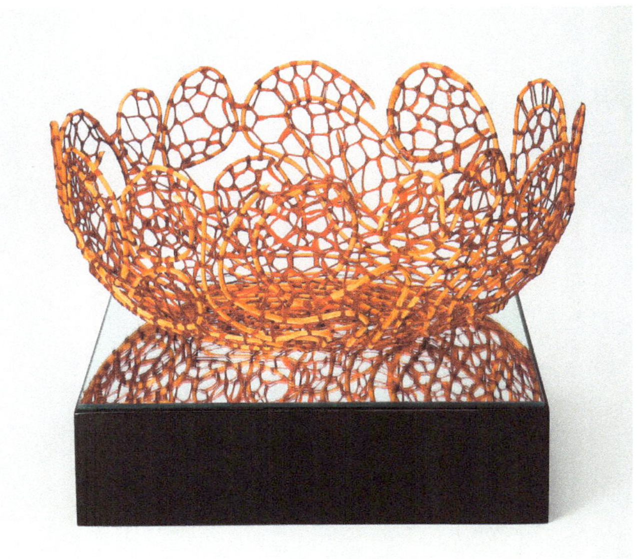

Although Clark's books present a wide variety of needle lace stitches based on embroidery stitches, in *Sepia Bowl* she relies on the most basic stitch, the simple buttonhole stitch, worked on vine rattan which forms the outline of the stitched areas in the manner of a cordonnette.

I usually work with stitched wet gut (casing) over a cylindrical or rectangular foamboard mold. The gut shrinks as it dries, then the mold is removed to reveal a free-standing lace like structure. *Sepia bowl* was my first experiment with shaped molds made from thick pink commercial insulating foam.

For *Sepia Bowl* I dyed the casing, then combined the stitched casing with dyed vine rattan purchased from a basketry supply company. Vine rattan when soaked in water is very flexible, and in this case, it creates a line drawing effect.

Jill Nordfors Clark. *Sepia Bowl,* 2009. Hog casing, needle lace, 6″ x 14.5″. Photo: Tom Holt.

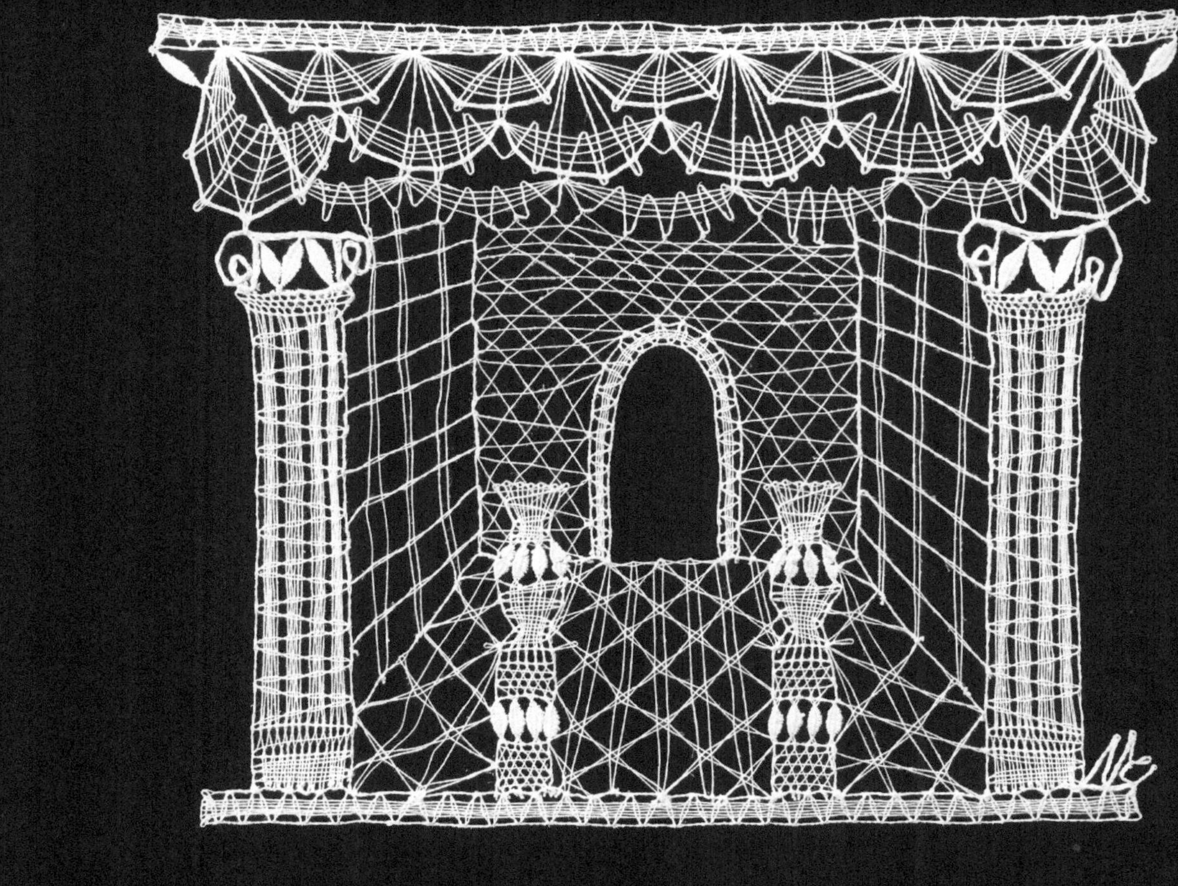

## Milča Eremiášová

Milča Eremiášová is one of the most important artists of the Czech modern lace movement. Her work spans the years from the mid-20th century until the present. Over this time she has made small pieces, large pieces, installations, and wearables. She has worked in white and in color, in two dimensions and in three dimensions, made representational art, and abstract art. She has many sources of inspiration, including music, the theatre, religious themes, and the sea.

Eremiášová was born in Prague in 1938 where she graduated from the College of Applied Arts having studied in the lacemaking and embroidery studio of professors Emilie Paličková and Antonín Kybal, where she later completed her postgraduate studies (1967-1971). From 1962 until 1995 she taught at the School Institute of Art Manufacturing in Prague. Between 1990 and 1995 she was the head of the lacemaking and embroidery studio at the privately-owned Master School of Art Design in Prague. She first received international recognition for her work with a series of lace wearables exhibited at the Montreal Expo in Canada in 1967. She has exhibited around the world, most notably Sweden and the Netherlands. Her works are represented in private and museum collections worldwide.[23]

We are fortunate to have four pieces of Eremiášová's work, from the collection of her student Dagmar Beckel-Machyckova. Beckel-Machyckova chose well, buying small pieces that are technically complex and artistically expressive. Eremiášová made many of these miniature pieces comparable to sketches, called chamber compositions. *Church of San Salvador* and *Fountain* are most likely part of her series about Prague architecture that she executed during the 1970s and 80s. *Small Theatre* dates from 1983 when Eremiášová exhibited over 30 theatre-based designs in the Czech city Hradec Králové. *Gothic Window,* a more recent work relates three of her frequent themes, architecture, religion and plants.

Milča Eremiášová. *Small Theater,* 1983. Bobbin lace, cotton, 7″ x 5″. Photo: Dagmar Beckel-Machyckova.

In *Fountain* and *Small Theatre* we see a sophisticated use of perspective. Eremiášová selects square based grounds distorting them to create the impression of depth. A close study of her work reveals a nuanced use of thread to make lines of varying widths or intensity from the single thread, to the twisted pair, to the use of plaits. The topics of these lace sketches are things that delight Eremiášová and, while very laborious to complete, convey a simple appreciation for beautiful things.

To me, bobbin lace is like brushes and paints to a painter. I constantly find new possibilities, both in the use of color, various textiles and materials as well as in lace structure. There are no longer restrictions, but the artist's touch has to maintain the tectonics and rules of the classic technique of bobbin lacemaking.[24]

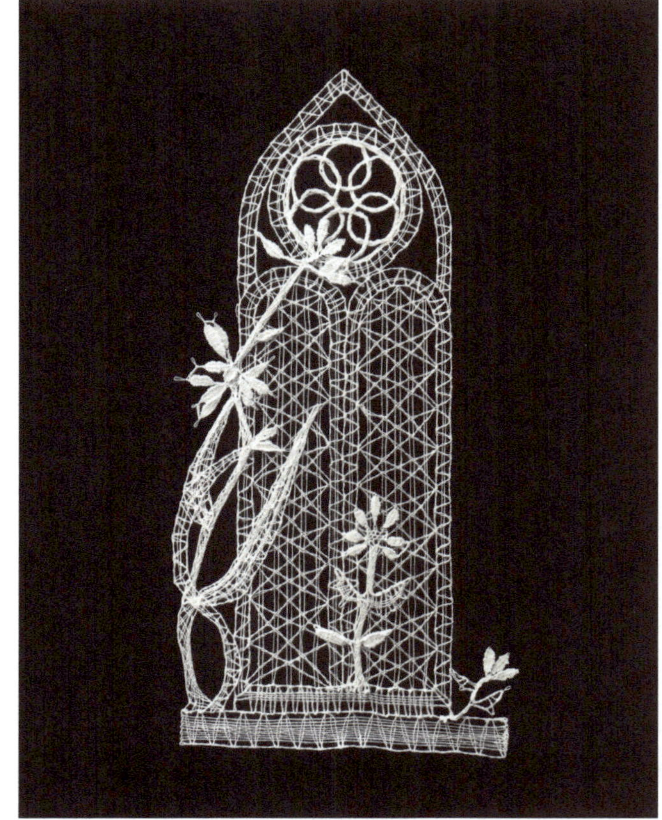

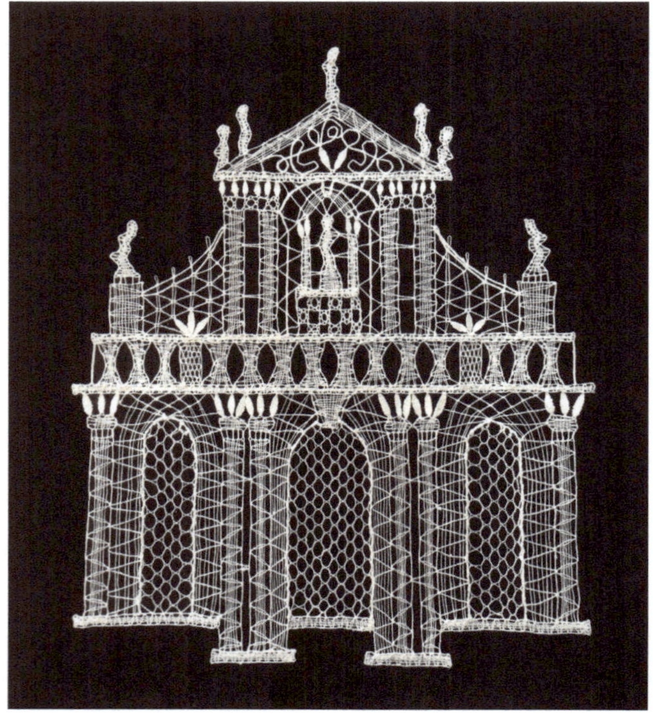

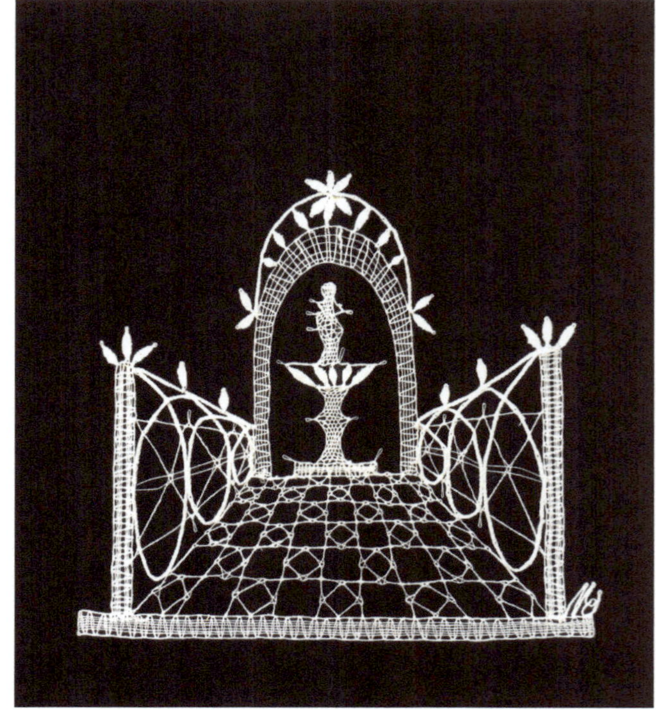

Milča Eremiášová.*Church of San Salvador.* 1974, Bobbin lace, cotton, 7 1/2" x 9". Photo: Dagmar Beckel-Machyckova.

Milča Eremiášová. *Gothic Window, 2015. Bobbin lace, cotton, 5" x 10". Photo: Dagmar Beckel-Machyckova.*

Milča Eremiášová. *Fountain, 1986. Bobbin lace, cotton, 6 1/2" x 6". Photo: Dagmar Beckel-Machyckova.*

## Pierre Fouché

South African artist Pierre Fouché earned his MA in Fine Arts from the University of Stellenbosch. He has had solo exhibitions in South Africa and Switzerland. He is often shown at the WHATIFTHEWORLD Gallery in Cape Town which represents him. His work has traveled to the United States to appear in the show *Queer Threads* at the Leslie+Lohman Museum in New York, and to Boston to appear in the exhibition *Crafted: Objects in Flux* at the Boston Museum of Fine Arts.

Fouché began his lace studies with books borrowed from the library, but then became acquainted with the Cape Lace Guild where he attended weekly meetings at the home of Charlotte Keen to make lace under "supervision". He still attends these meetings and reports, "The informal way skills get transferred through craft circles is much more effective than learning from books. Intergenerational interaction is spiritually very nourishing too. I now consider Charlotte and the ladies from the Friday group my mentors and dear friends."

Fouché's work has been met with great enthusiasm by lacemakers who admire his consummate mastery of technique. Within *Judgment of Paris II* can be found a "snowflake" ground stretching over the left side of the figure's torso from waist to shoulder. The snowflake ground and its innumerable variations is a basic building block of Flemish laces of the 17th and 18th centuries. The snowflake, which looks like a ball, is a structure in which six pairs of thread meet, work a ball, then exit. Sometimes it is used as a "depot" that changes the route or direction of the pairs. The background mesh for *Judgment of Paris II* is a new version of the snowflake ground that was designed by Ulrike Löhr Voelcker as part of a class in designing grounds that she taught in Germany in the 1990s.[25] Fouché confesses that he finds it fun to try out interesting grounds, historical or newly designed. He believes that the background mesh is based on an historic ground found in the 18th century Flemish lace called Mechlin to which Voelcker has added a "chaotic" halo border that appeals to him.[26]

Technically, the most notable thing about Fouché's work is the unique way that he combines bobbin lace with macramé.

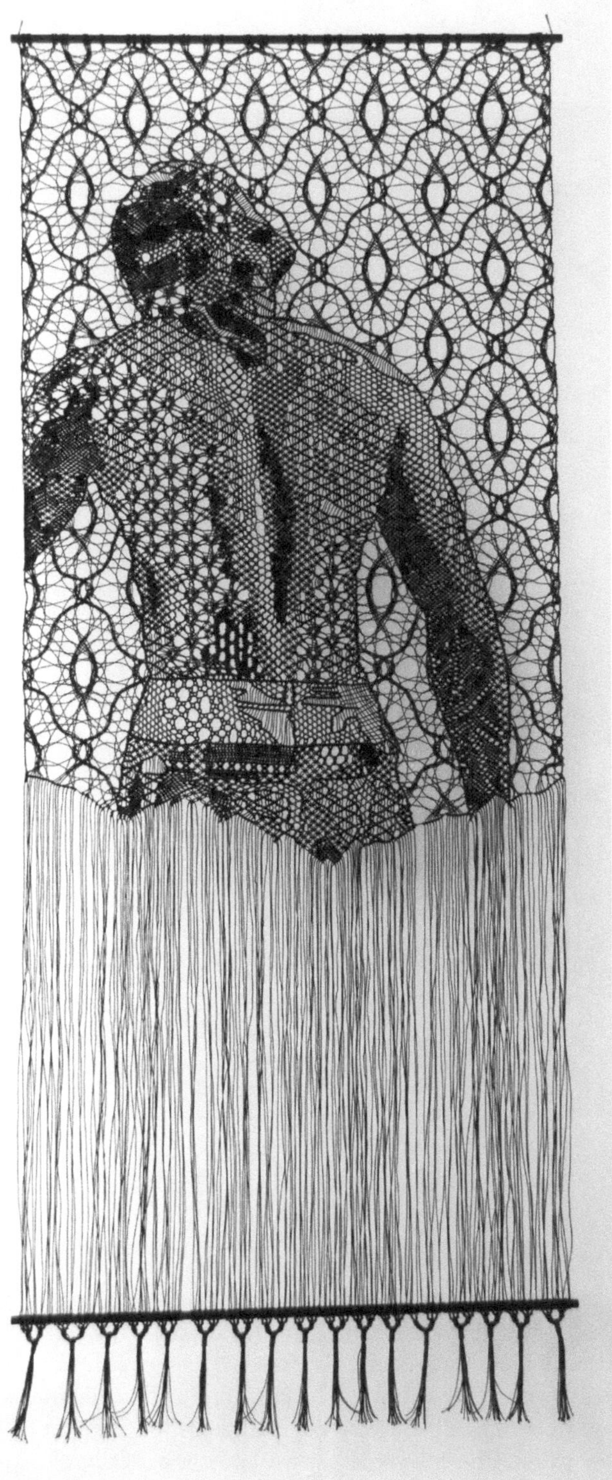

Pierre Fouché. *The Judgment of Paris (after Wtewael) II.*, 2015. Bobbin lace and macramé in polyester braid, 2.6′ x 6.5′.

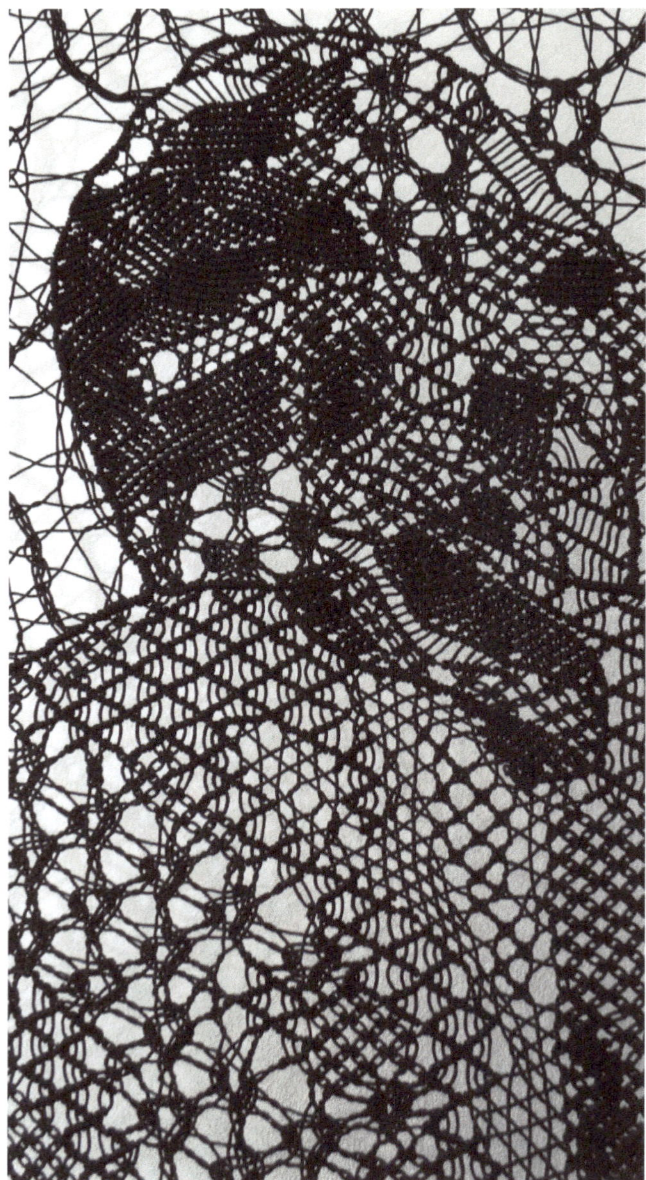

Pierre Fouché. *The Judgment of Paris (after Wtewael) II.* Detail.

Macramé is a knotting technique of ancient origin which has played an important role in the decoration of fringes and warp threads and is considered part of the canon of lacemaking techniques. It was widely practiced in the 16th and 17th centuries.[27] According to Fouché, macramé and bobbin lace are very compatible as long as you "think in pairs". The macramé square knot is basically two pairs intersecting.

Describing his design process, Fouché says:

*With macramé combined with bobbin lace I've arrived at a tonal range of 6 tones that can be applied like "pixels" at any crossing of two pairs. This is particularly useful to modulate detail areas like faces and hands. Where larger shapes of tones need to appear, I prefer to use more elaborate grounds to create a more interesting "painterly" texture in the lace. With these I don't always get the tone exactly right, but it is still better than having a very mechanical-looking, even ground. These remind me of digital glitches in certain jpegs, and in turn, of the digital origin of many of the images I use.*

I've always been drawn to craft and other amateur creative leisure pastimes due to the techniques' marginality to contemporary art. I find this marginality analogous to my work's engagement with the visual cultures and the psyche of non-normative sexuality.

The *Judgment of Paris (after Wtewael)* series exemplifies this. The work is the second panel of a triptych depicting the goddesses of the myth as contemporary male protestors, and it is made with a combination of bobbin lace weaving, and macramé knotwork techniques. The series is inspired by the precedents of the myth's depiction in the academic tradition: the subject conveniently allowed the representation of three female nudes. The source images for the bobbin lace and macramé panels were appropriated from web based news platforms, each selected for the classical references of their pose (and a personal affinity to the occupy-movement in two of the three panels).

On a broader level the work engages the politics of nudity and display; our positive (and negative) reactions to exhibitionism; our participation in it as consumers of visual culture and the mixed messages we are fed about the human body and its display. The work is about the iconography of sexual deviancy and the few but significant arenas of human interaction where male nudity is "permissible". It traces the iconography of the male nude in contemporary visual culture, and confirms their poses as imprinted to our muscle memory by the visual repertoire of history.

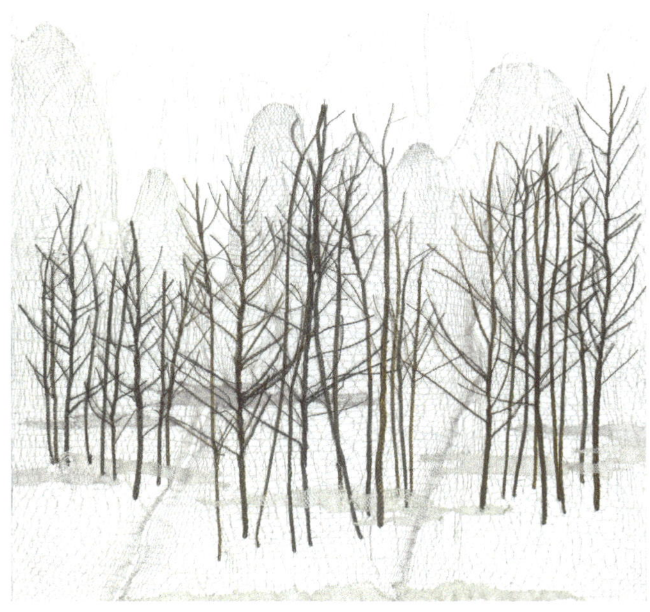

## Laura Friesel

Laura Friesel describes her art as "lace painting". Determined to see bobbin lace take its place as fine art, her work is design driven. Lace techniques and fiber choices are made in the service of the design.

Friesel comes from a family of lacemakers who emigrated from the English Midlands, a region known for handmade lace production.[28] Her great-grandmother and great-aunts were lacemakers. Friesel's mother studied Milanese tape lace with a prominent lacemaker from Milan, Italy. When she was 13 years old, Friesel begged her mother to teach her how to make Milanese lace, which she found to be fascinating. After the fall of the Berlin Wall in 1989, Friesel realized that her career as a Russian translator for the Air Force was at an end, allowing her to return to her lace studies with her mother. She also studied with Holly Van Sciver, an expert in English laces who was an important figure in the US lace revival of the 1970s.

Friesel appreciates the unique properties of lace which can be very solid or very airy. She likes to combine different lace styles with interesting fibers, cotton, linen, silk and wire, to create a range of effects from refreshingly contemporary to subtly traditional. In *Winter*, a piece inspired by a 12th Century poem by Minamoto no Sanetomo, she has combined two very different materials: metal and silk. The winter trees are braided of fine gauge silver wire oxidized with sulfur creating dark, rugged, three-dimensional trunks. A gossamer fine silk floss is used for the fog and mist. Behind the trees the fog is formed by layers of pinless point ground. The under-lying layer, farther in the distance, is worked in larger, looser, more erratic stitches, while the fog in the middle ground is more tightly worked, but also without the regulating function of pins. Half stitch patches of fog rise among the trees, giving the appearance of an enveloping mist, sometimes passing in front of the trunks, sometimes behind. In this piece Friesel has shown her mastery of layering and transparency.

The nature of lace involves a balance between the solid thread and the open spaces that give the fabric its "lacyness". I find that the Japanese aesthetic is perfect for taking that search for balance to the image itself as I explore harmony in asymmetry.

I take my inspiration from classical Japanese court poetry written roughly between the eighth and twelfth centuries. In keeping with my inspiration, my aesthetic is firmly rooted in Japanese art and its symbolism. Even in works that are not obviously Japanese inspired, like *Winter*, I pay close attention to the balance of filled and empty space.

*Winter*
*Autumn's gone away,*
*The wind has blown from the trees*
*every single leaf;*
*and the mountains are forlorn*
*now that winter has come*
*-Minamoto no Sanetomo*

Laura Friesel. *Winter*, 2013. Bobbin lace, 18 3/4″ x 18 3/4″. Photo: Jen Shu.

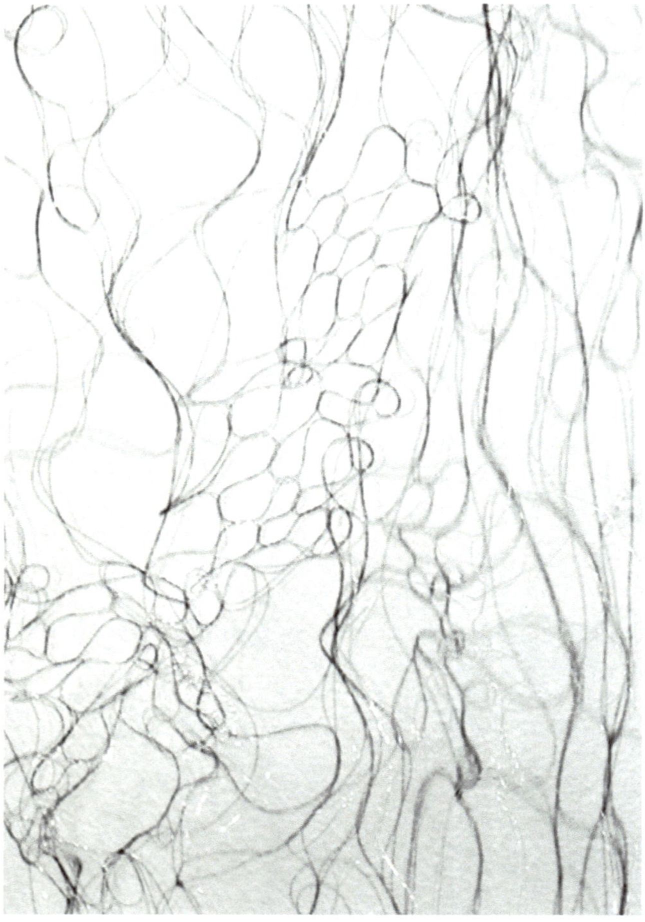

## Alex Goldberg

Describing herself as a lover of lace, Alex Goldberg says she wore a lot of lace when she was a child. After studying Art History and Drawing at Boston University, she went to graduate school at Pratt Institute to study Interior Design. Her graduate thesis dealt with soft nomadic interiors which led her to the Textile Arts Center, a Brooklyn and Manhattan based textile education facility where she immersed herself in learning different textile practices. There she became interested in studying lace and became a member of the Brooklyn Lace Guild.

Goldberg was attracted to bobbin lace as a method for creating shadows in that it has so many openings. She taught herself the skill from YouTube instructional videos and from pattern books, including *Bobbin Lace Making*[29] by Doris Southard, a book originally published in 1977 which deals mostly with Torchon lace. *Olive* and *Bishop's Mitre* patterns were taken from the book *100 Traditional Bobbin Lace Patterns*[30] by Geraldine Stott and Bridget Cook. Published in 1982 this is a book in which the authors painstakingly copied traditional 19th century British Bucks Point patterns, producing prickings[31] and colored diagrams denoting stitches so that they could be worked again. Bucks Point was a lace made in Buckinghamshire with a point ground mesh. Many of the patterns were taken from the *Lace Dealer's Pattern Book*, a sample book of lace that contains pieces of lace being sold between 1854 to 1893. The sample book is in the collection of the Luton Museum.[32]

Goldberg worked the patterns in large scale and in transparent monofilament thread, commonly known as "invisible thread", which deforms in unexpected ways. At first the work appears disorderly and abstract, but on close examination one can detect the repetitive pattern of the Bucks Point edging. Thus, a serviceable 19th century lace border is delivered into a 21st century art work through the mediation of members of the late 20th century lace revival.

*Invisible Place* is a conceptual textile and light installation that explores the intangible aspects of our reality. From the furthest glance it will appear as if there is nothing there, but a closer study will reveal quiet intricate design. The viewer's experience of discovering the intricacies in the work mimics the experience of getting to know someone or learning about something. Each of the works, created from a 19th century bobbin lace pattern, uses unconventional material and scale bringing the unknown into the equation. The pattern acts as a map for the process, yet the outcome is never fully predictable. Just like our experience of living, it is unclear what the piece will become until the process is over and the lace is unpinned and taken off the pattern. The lacework is faint and traced by its own shadow. It appears to be absent from the physical world until it is activated by light. From afar the lacework is invisible, but the further the viewer moves into the installation the more intricacies are revealed. This experience mirrors the experience of getting to know someone or something in the way that people make initial judgements and then later truths and complexities are revealed. While that process could take years, this experience is a speedy simulation of these feelings of wonder and surprise. Rewarding the careful and patient "listener," *Invisible Place* is an ode to the often overlooked.

Alex Goldberg. *Invisible Place*, 2016. Monofilament thread, 144″ x 168″.

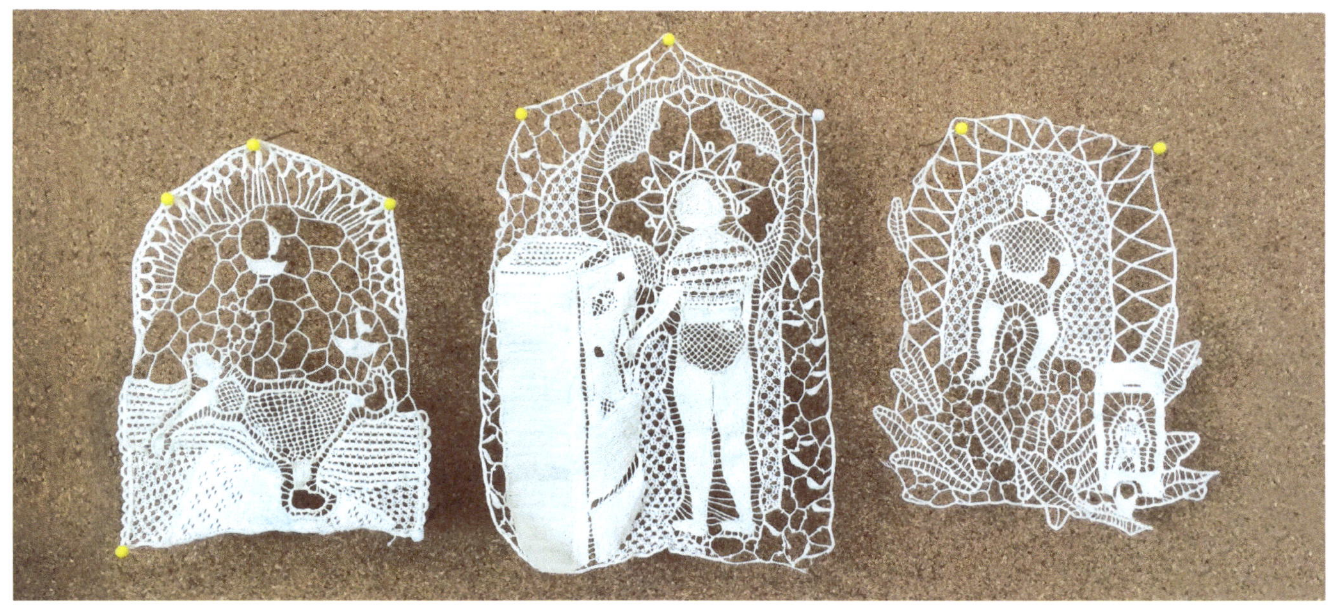

## Maggie Hensel-Brown

Australian artist Maggie Hensel-Brown received her Fine Arts degree from the University of Newcastle in New South Wales. In 2015 she stumbled on a class in *reticella* with Margaret Stephens at the Australian Lace Guild's annual general meeting in Melbourne and was "immediately hooked". She loves the way techniques change slightly according to geography and history. Her technique combines *punto in aria*, Venetian *gros point* and Aemilia Ars. In *punto in aria* lace made the leap from using a framework derived by pulling threads from a piece of woven fabric (*reticella*) to true needle lace where the framework is laid onto a parchment pattern and held down with couching stitches. Venetian *gros point*, a heavy baroque needle lace of the 17th century followed *punto in aria* chronologically. Aemilia Ars was a 19th and early 20th century revival lace in which the techniques of punto in aria were imitated.[33]

A contemporary aesthetic infuses Hensel-Brown's tiny guipure vignettes. Guipure lace is lace in which the motifs are connected by bars. It predates mesh-based laces which became the norm in the 18th century. In *Coping Mechanism II*, the surface under the reclining figure recalls diamond shaped patterns commonly found in *gros point*, while the roughly hexagonal background resonates with the transition from guipure laces to grounded laces by way of the hexagonal ground of *point de France*. The subtly curving corded buttonhole stitch that forms the solid areas of the figures suggests musculature in the male figure, and even a certain incipient chubbiness in *Staring into the Void*. The contrast of curving lines of stitching in some areas juxtaposed against more linear stitching is a characteristic that often enlivened and enriched the robust laces of the 17th century and Hensel-Brown has made good use of them in her work.

Hensel-Brown's work has been particularly influenced by a number of 17th century needle lace pieces depicting the Biblical story of Judith and Holofernes. In these the Jewish heroine beheads the Assyrian King with the help of Abra her maid. A needle lace version of this story in the collection of the Powerhouse Museum in Sydney incorporates human hair in the coiffures of the characters and in the beard of Holofernes. Red thread is introduced to articulate the aortic

Maggie Hensel-Brown. *Coping Mechanism II: Get Stoned and Watch Boats*, 2016. Cotton, needle lace, 4.7″ x 3.9″

*Staring into the Void: Not Hungry, Just Bored*, 2016-2017. Silk, needle lace, 4.7″ x 6.3″

*Dancing the Dance of a Special Boy for Sixty Seconds or Less*, 2017. Silk, needle lace, 4.7″ x 3.9″

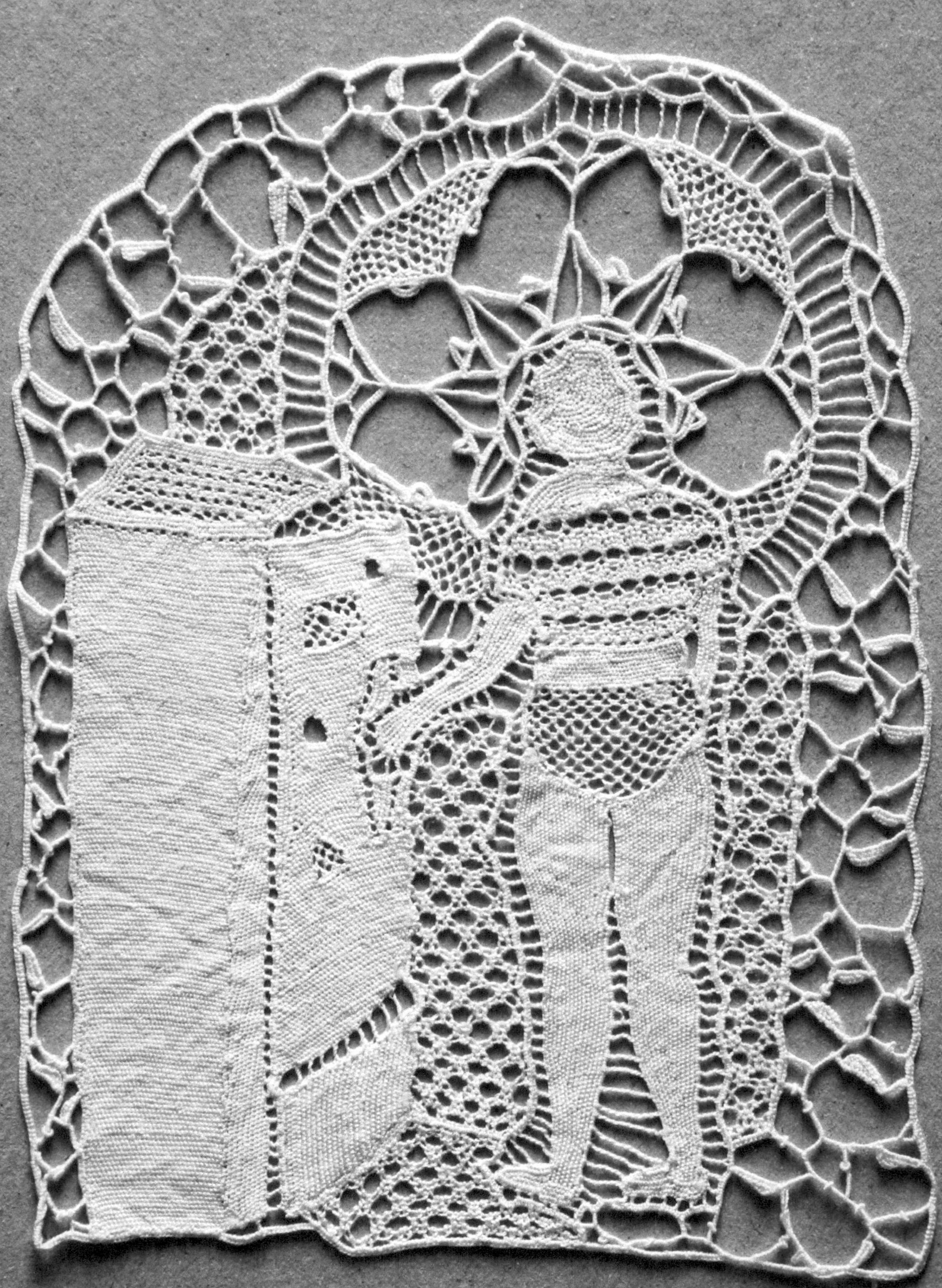

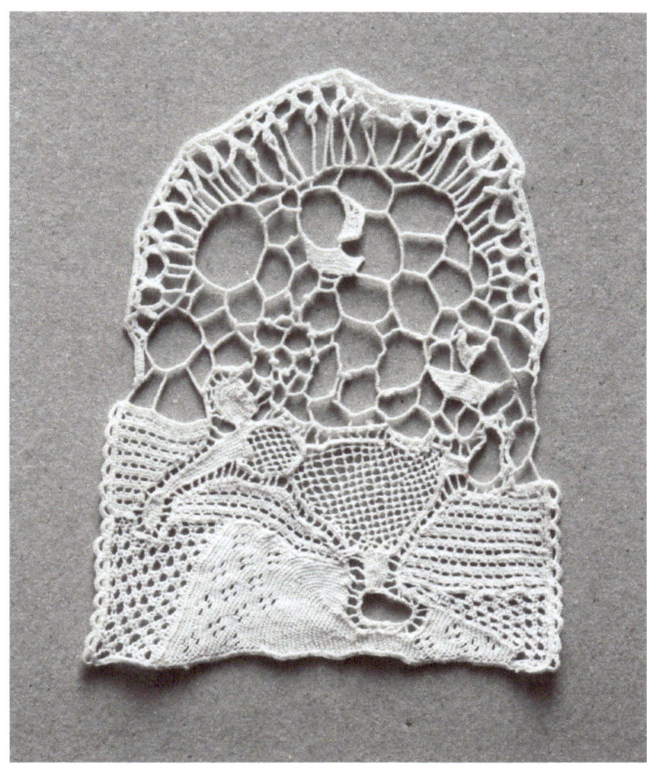

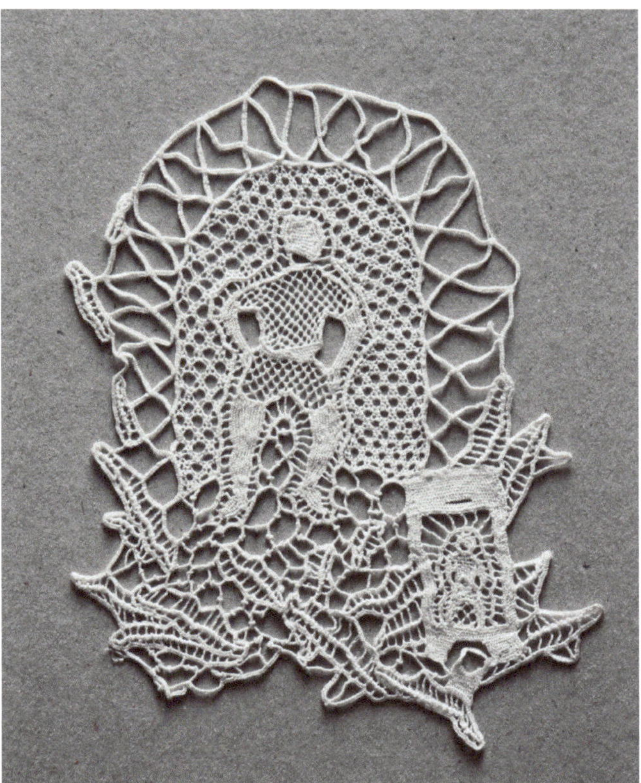

blood spurting from the headless torso.[34] The version of the story in the Metropolitan Museum of Art is chronologically earlier and more solid in style, but the lacemakers proved equally able to depict gore in needle lace.[35]

Inspired by these examples and others depicting heroic scenes, Hensel-Brown chooses to depict unremarkable moments that nonetheless have a certain universality to them.

There is a combination of lightness and gravity in needle lace that I am fascinated by, and I love the way it continues to surprise me with new layers of intricacy.

My subject matter stems mostly from tiny, ordinary moments in my own life. The research I've done into pictorial needle lace shows mostly images from biblical tales or grand moments in the life of the gentry. I love the idea of taking a process so labour intensive and so historically intertwined with grandeur and turning it on its head. Therefore, my imagery generally shows life at the height of its ordinariness.

The three pieces in this show range from frustration to despondency to quiet moments of joy. The first, *Coping Mechanism II: Get Stoned and Watch Boats* comes from a recent family trip and my incredibly flawed manner of dealing with intense and entrenched family dynamics. The second, *Staring into the Void, Not Hungry, Just Bored* comes from the height of an Australian summer when I was unemployed and uninspired, spending days eating snacks and reading novels. Finally, in *Dancing the Dance of a Special Boy for Sixty Seconds or Less*, I'm trying to show the joy I feel while silently giggling and trying not to drop the camera while my brother dances beautifully and hilariously for an Instagram film.

For me, needle lace is a way to slowly, intricately and painstakingly meditate on life and the world around me. It is also a chance to feel like a part of a long history of creative, methodical and talented women who have finely crafted their techniques for centuries.

Maggie Hensel-Brown. *Staring into the Void: Not Hungry, Just Bored.*

Maggie Hensel-Brown. *Coping Mechanism II: Get Stoned and Watch Boats.*

Maggie Hensel-Brown. *Dancing the Dance of a Special Boy for Sixty Seconds or Less.*

## Ágnes Herczeg

Hungarian artist Agnes Herczeg studied textile conservation at the Hungarian University of Fine Arts. However, from the beginning, she was interested in the process of creating art rather than simply restoring it. She wanted to learn about almost-forgotten techniques such as lacemaking. Herczeg makes small pieces often showing women in positions of work or contemplation. Each takes several days to complete. Herczeg has found that making these pieces and selling them over the internet is a satisfying artistic practice that is compatible with her life as the mother of a large family.

The artist admires Mária Markovits, inventor of Halas lace. Halas lace is a Hungarian lace industry originally formed in 1902 as part of the Vienna Secession artistic movement. Subject matter for the earliest Halas lace included Hungarian peasants in national costume and typical Hungarian flowers and animals such as deer, doves and peacocks. Many of the early pieces were in color. While Árpád Dékáni and Antal Tar were male designers who are credited with the success of the venture, Mária Markovits was the technical expert who invented the Halas lace technique. In Halas lace, the solid areas, or cloth work is achieved by weaving with a needle. This laborious process when finished looks like a finely woven cambric has been inserted in the piece. But instead the fabric has been woven to the shape of the motif. The gossamer cloth area is surrounded by a thick thread to emphasize the outline of the motif. Background stitching in very fine thread incorporates a startling variety of buttonhole-based needle lace stitches.[36]

Although she reveres Markovits, in her work, Herczeg is more directly inspired by prehistoric artists. She uses only natural materials of vegetable origin, including wood, clay and coconut shells. Herczeg incorporates needle lace, bobbin lace and braiding in her work. In *II-34*, a piece that is built into the crook of a small twig, a woman looks out through an unevenly braided lace curtain which merges with the figure's skirt creating a *trompe l'oeil* effect. Linen and hemp are used in variations of four strand braiding, transitioning into large, loose multistrand braids before dividing into a fringe of narrow, tight, four strand braids. While the background is braided, the figure's torso, arms and head are needle lace, outlined in thin copper wire. The wire is covered with buttonhole stitches in cotton thread. Herczeg uses rows of buttonhole stitches of even height to create linear accents, but then employs a form of interlacing to fill uneven design areas. In a departure from the usual practice in lacemaking, Herczeg is not afraid to use a paint brush to apply additional color and nuance to the surface of her works.

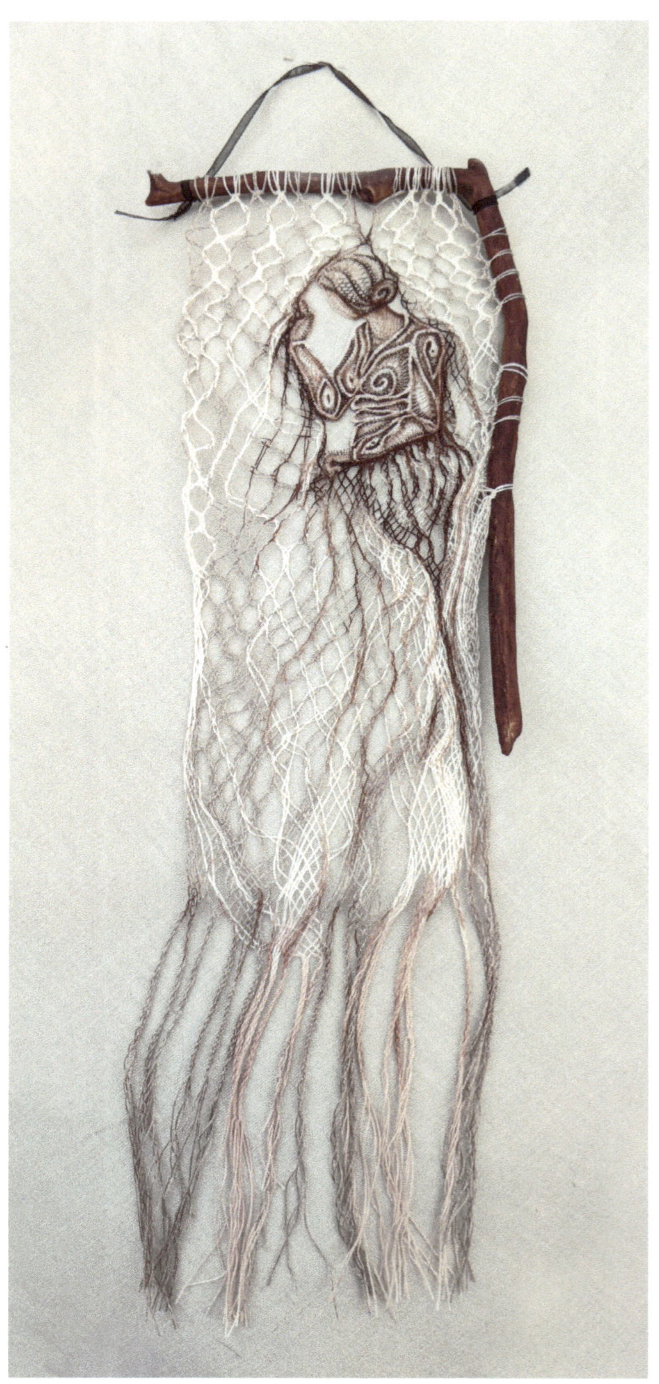

Ágnes Herczeg. *II-34*, 2015. Bobbin and needle lace, 17 3/4″ x 6 1/4″. Photo: Peggy Lagodny

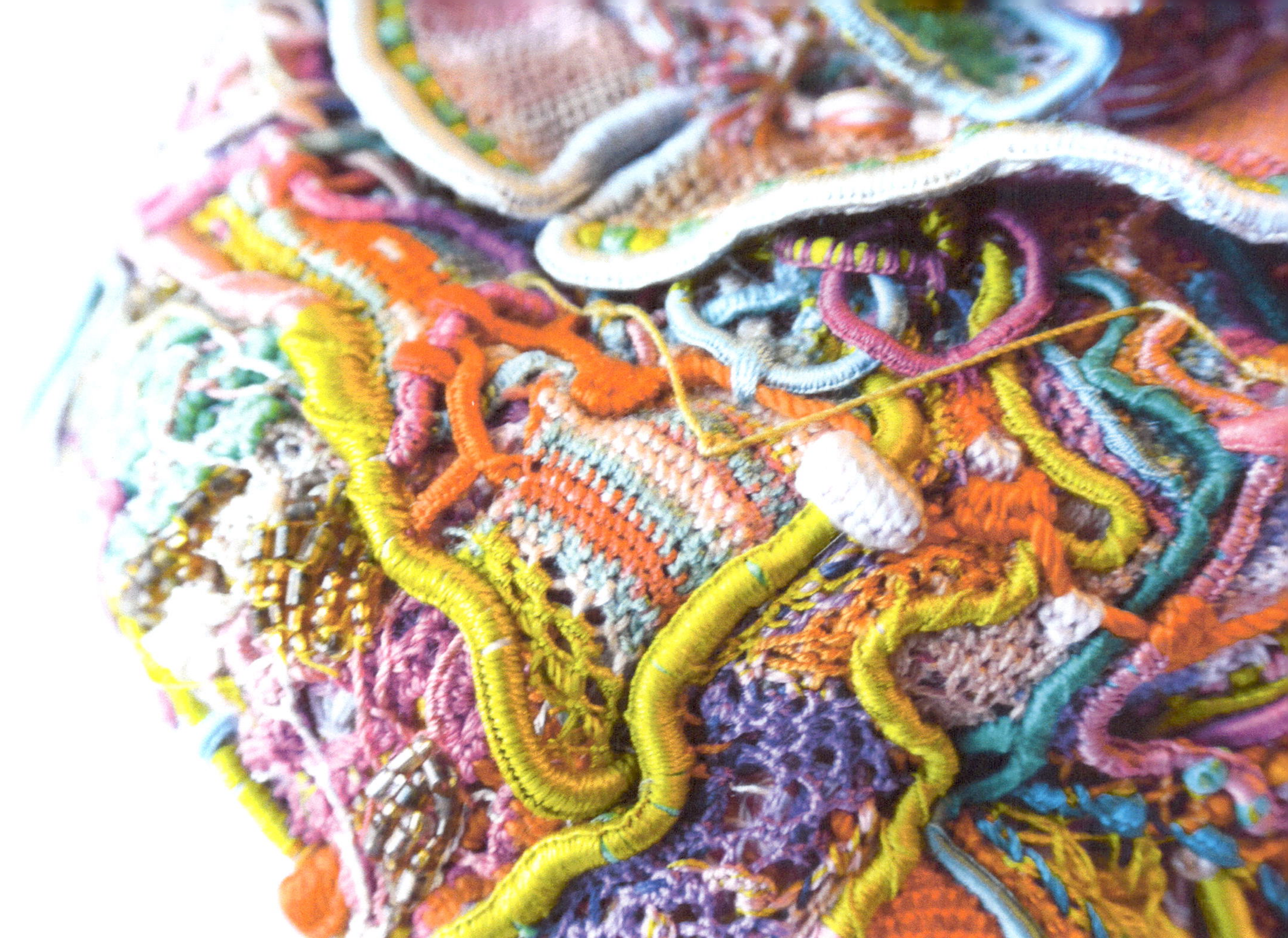

## Ros Hills

When the Victoria and Albert Museum decided that it would like to purchase a piece of contemporary needle lace in 1986, it bought a small needle lace purse made by artist Ros Hills. [37] We are fortunate to be able to exhibit a similar purse made in the same time period that the artist kept in her personal collection.

Ros Hills learned needle lace at a City and Guilds of London textile course. She immediately enjoyed needle lace as a way of constructing a fabric using only needle and thread. The technique seemed to offer infinite possibilities as a medium of expression.

Hills' specialty was creative needle lace with a late 20th century aesthetic. In her book *Colour and Texture in Needlelace*,[38] published in 1987 she advocates the needle lacemaker collect interesting threads whenever possible so that she may have a multitude of choices of color and texture. She even includes a chapter on dying threads if appropriately colored threads are not available. A childhood spent in Iraq, India and the Caribbean informs Hills' color choices which are as vibrant and unrestrained as her designs. Ribbon, metallic thread, beads and sequins are often included in her work to give it extra sparkle.[39] Despite the fact that Hills coauthored a book with Pat Gibson, *Needlelace Stitches: Classic and Contemporary*[40] which contains many different stitches, Hills prefers to use very simple needle lace techniques, relying on color and texture for effect.

In *Purse 2* and *I am Woman* (based on a cap worn by Indian women) Hills relies on tight corded buttonhole stitch to make a solid fabric on which to work her textural magic. Her approach is reminiscent of 17th century *gros point* in which a solid fabric was created primarily with corded buttonhole stitches, relying on padded condonets covered with close stitching called cordonnette for exuberantly baroque ornamentation. The cordonnette can be conducted in spiral configurations, decorated with loops and picots, and spaced to reveal the inner padding threads.[41]

Ros Hills. *I am Woman.* Detail

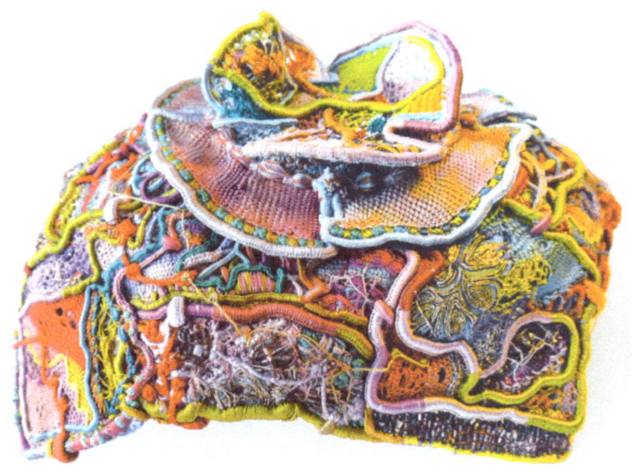

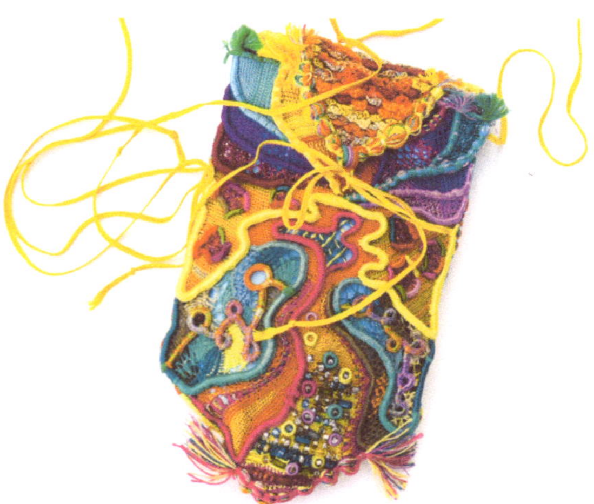

In both pieces Hills makes use of exposed padding threads of contrasting color in the cordonet. These multi-thread "paddings" protrude in soft puffs between the tightly stitched areas of the cordonnette. For the most part the artist does not use tapered hugely padded cordonets such as was common in *gros point*. Instead a hallmark of her work are cordonets of even width that run sinuously along the surface of the work. Small couronnes (buttonholed rings) are worked around cordonets or strewn across the surface of the piece.

Lace was/is often worn on special occasions when societal ritual is performed. The desire to decorate and enhance the performers in the ritual would seem to be embedded, the cleansing of body and mind and the putting on of special clothing and or bodily decoration would seem to be a strong part of such rituals. Such clothing takes on a great importance within family groups and can be handed down through generations. Lace has played its part in these rituals.

When designing the suite of four purses, of which *Purse 2* was one, and also *I Am Woman* the cap, I wanted to celebrate not only the lives of female lacemakers of the past but also to make a statement about women's lives in general in all its complexity and diversity hence the mixed areas of stitching, color and texture in both pieces. I envisaged the pieces being worn/used on ritualistic occasions to enhance that occasion and the wearer, I wanted to push the boundaries in terms of lace design.

Ros Hills. *I am Woman,* 1987. Needle lace, silk thread and beads, 3″ x 7″ x 7″. Photo: Ros Hills.

Ros Hills. *Purse 2,* 1985. Needle lace, silk thread and beads, 5 1/2″ x 3 1/2″. Photo: Ros Hills.

Ros Hills. *Purse 2.* Detail.

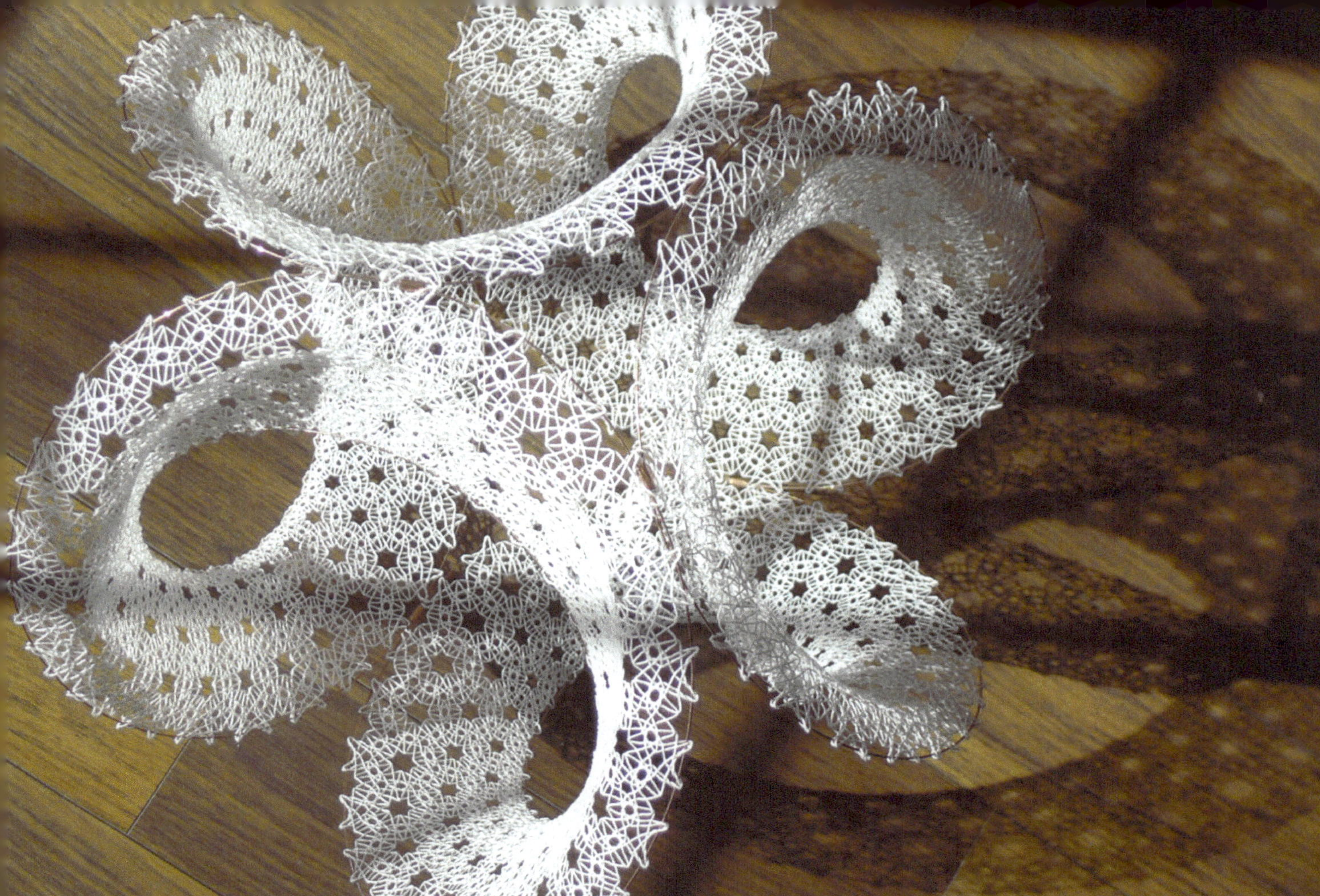

## Veronika Irvine

Lacemaking is very mathematical. Lace making machines, run on Jacquard technology, were arguably the first computers. Lace grounds of the 17th and 18th century show an astounding mathematical complexity, although made by an entirely illiterate workforce. So, it is not surprising that a mathematician would be drawn to lacemaking. Veronika Irvine's Ph.D. dissertation, *Lace Tessellations: A mathematical model for bobbin lace and an exhaustive combinatorial search for patterns*[42] is a fascinating development in lacemaking. Through the power of modern computer technology she has generated over 5 million lace ground patterns, whereas her research into historical ground patterns reveals only about 1000 in existence.

The new grounds have a sleek 21st century look. Irvine has identified some of the most aesthetically pleasing grounds and has begun to explore them artistically. She works in white, which serves to signal that the work is "lace". *Bee Prepared* and *Triaxial Arrow Heads* present the ground alone, in a frame. In traditional lace design, the ground is secondary to the motif. In fact, grounds developed in the late 17th century to create negative space around increasingly small motifs. But in Irvine's work the ground has become the focus, and there are no motifs. In *Delle Caustiche*, Irvine makes the leap into three dimensions and produces a sculptural piece with a sound mathematical pedigree. Irvine's fusion of mathematics and textile art is as exciting as it is inevitable.[43]

Veronika Irvine. *Delle Caustiche*, 2017. White cotton thread, copper wire, handmade bobbin lace, 10″ x 15″ x 15″.

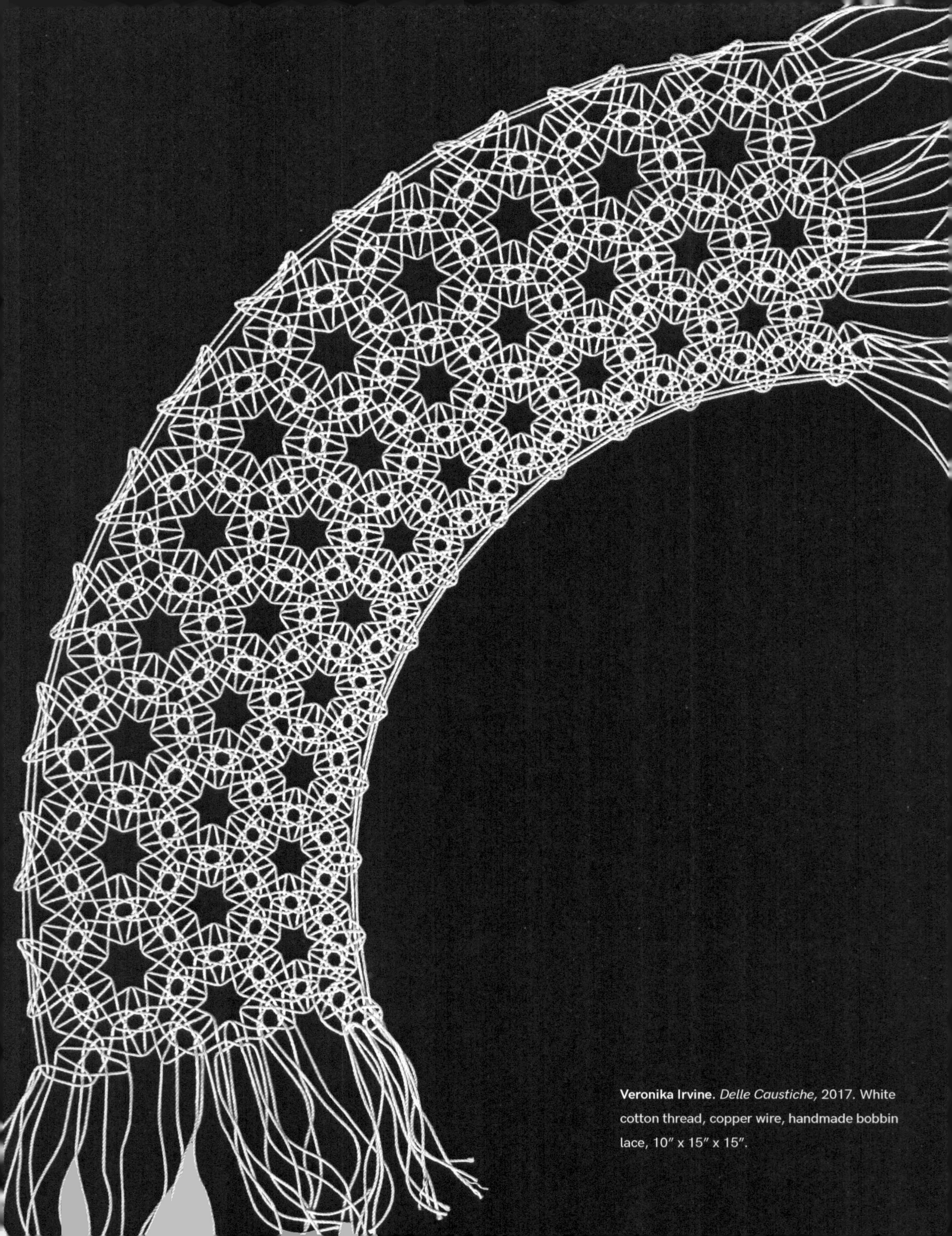

**Veronika Irvine.** *Delle Caustiche,* 2017. White cotton thread, copper wire, handmade bobbin lace, 10″ x 15″ x 15″.

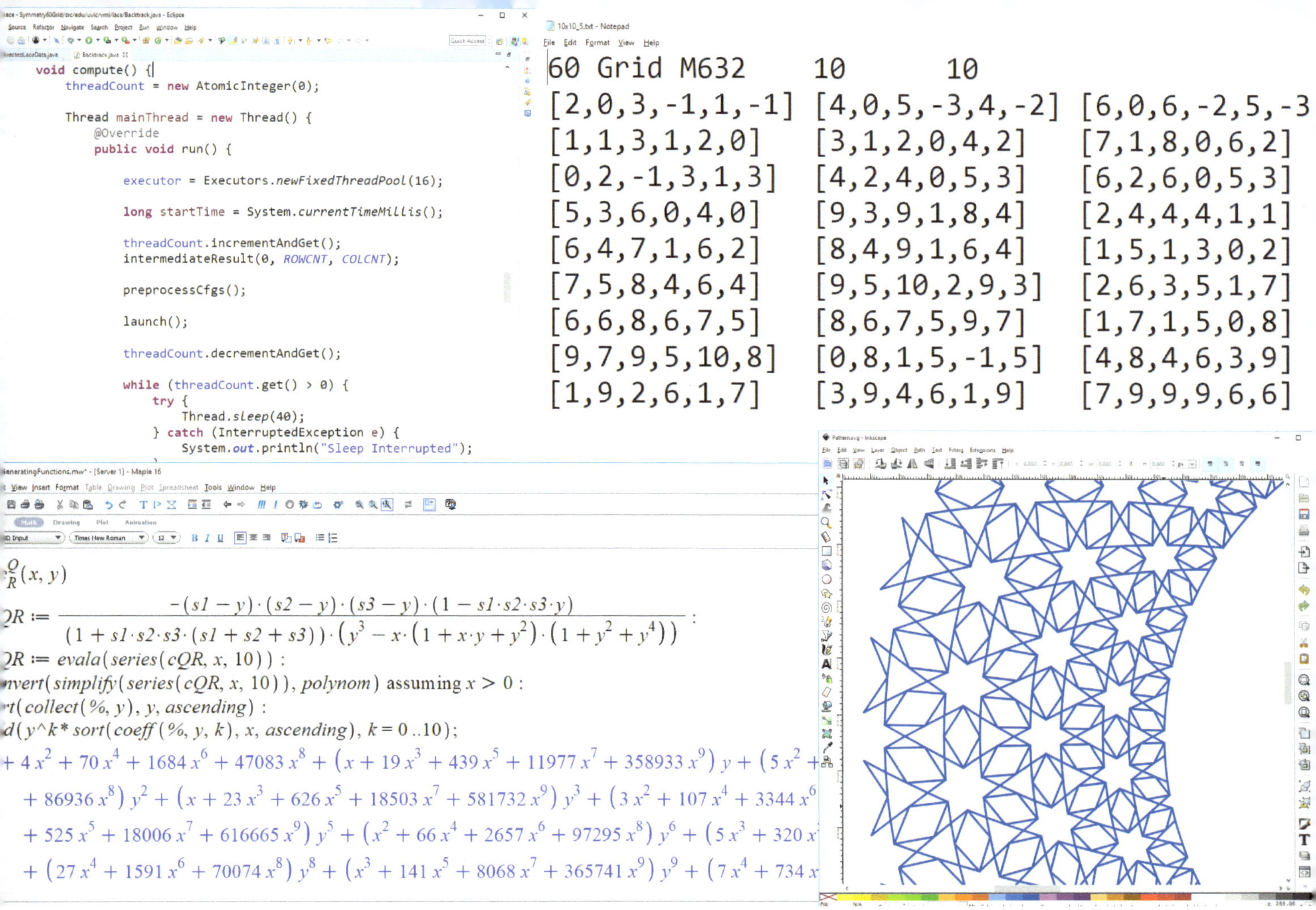

```
void compute() {
    threadCount = new AtomicInteger(0);

    Thread mainThread = new Thread() {
        @Override
        public void run() {

            executor = Executors.newFixedThreadPool(16);

            long startTime = System.currentTimeMillis();

            threadCount.incrementAndGet();
            intermediateResult(0, ROWCNT, COLCNT);

            preprocessCfgs();

            launch();

            threadCount.decrementAndGet();

            while (threadCount.get() > 0) {
                try {
                    Thread.sleep(40);
                } catch (InterruptedException e) {
                    System.out.println("Sleep Interrupted");
```

```
60 Grid M632     10     10
[2,0,3,-1,1,-1] [4,0,5,-3,4,-2] [6,0,6,-2,5,-3
[1,1,3,1,2,0]   [3,1,2,0,4,2]   [7,1,8,0,6,2]
[0,2,-1,3,1,3]  [4,2,4,0,5,3]   [6,2,6,0,5,3]
[5,3,6,0,4,0]   [9,3,9,1,8,4]   [2,4,4,4,1,1]
[6,4,7,1,6,2]   [8,4,9,1,6,4]   [1,5,1,3,0,2]
[7,5,8,4,6,4]   [9,5,10,2,9,3]  [2,6,3,5,1,7]
[6,6,8,6,7,5]   [8,6,7,5,9,7]   [1,7,1,5,0,8]
[9,7,9,5,10,8]  [0,8,1,5,-1,5]  [4,8,4,6,3,9]
[1,9,2,6,1,7]   [3,9,4,6,1,9]   [7,9,9,9,6,6]
```

Since early childhood, I have been drawn to creating objects from fibers of any kind: wool, thread, cloth, straw, wire, to name a few. My first memorable encounter with lace occurred when I was five years old. On my mother's dresser was a small pile of tatted lace fragments. I spent hours trying to figure out how the pieces were supposed to connect together. In some places the tiny knots were falling apart, revealing more about their structure and leading me to wonder how they had been formed. Many years later, I found out that these fragments came from the outer ring of a doily which my grandmother had been working on when she passed away at the age of 35. A relative had cut off and discarded the unfinished bits and kept the center. While it saddens me to reflect on the reason why these pieces were not joined together, the fact that they came into my life in this unfinished, disconnected state is what attracted my attention and held my interest – I was engaged in imagining the process and piecing together the puzzle. At the age of 10, I taught myself how to tat from a library book. In my mid-20s, I joined the Ottawa Guild of Lacemakers and learned the fundamentals of bobbin lace from Gail Young and Malvary Cole.

I am a computer scientist and a lacemaker. From my very first lesson in bobbin lace, I was struck by the logical yet complex nature of the art form. It inspired me to want to capture the essence of bobbin lace in a mathematical model. I started by representing the repeating fillings or grounds using braid theory and graph theory. From this abstract, mathematical generalization, I was able to write a computer program to generate millions of bobbin lace ground patterns. In particular, I have focused on patterns with symmetries that are relatively rare or unknown in traditional practice, symmetries such as six and three-fold mirrors and rotations. The pieces in this exhibit are examples of my algorithmically discovered (but realised by hand) patterns. The piece *Delle Caustiche* takes the study of symmetry one step further. Here, not only does the pattern have an unusual symmetry (described as *632/632 two-color orbifold symmetry, in math parlance), the whole shape of the piece is a study in three-dimensional symmetry.

Veronika Irvine. *Delle Caustiche.* Process.

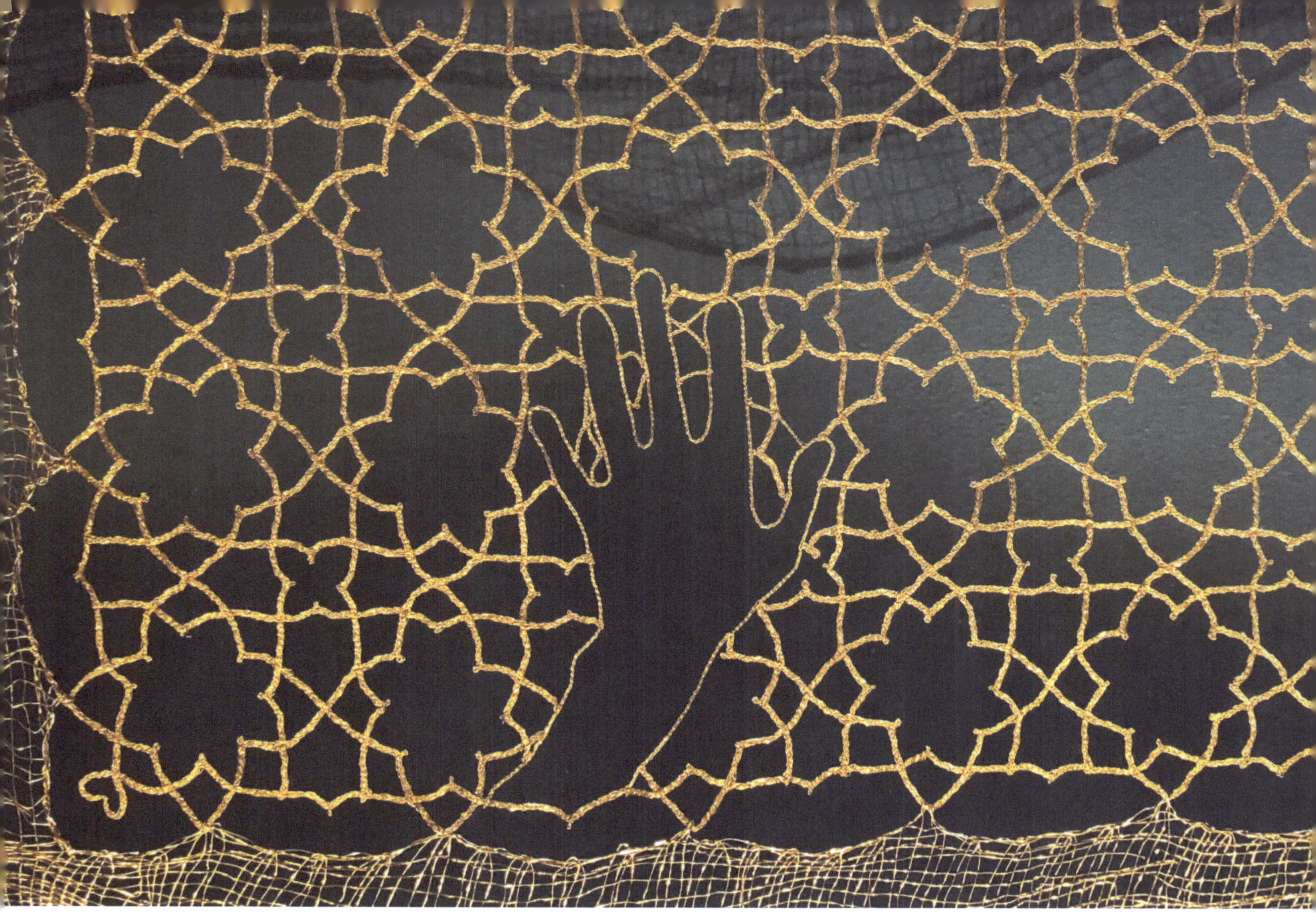

## Lieve Jerger

It is a privilege to present the first museum exhibition of Lieve Jerger's Carriage of Lost Love. This life size carriage has been under construction since 1977 and is still not finished. In fact, changes in artistic style are visible within the piece. The original panels which form the windows were made in the 1970s and resonate with the San Francisco vibe of that era. The wheels, the most recent additions, are less obviously emotive, but convey the mature spirituality of the artist and the solace that she derives from the natural world.

Lieve Jerger. *The Carriage of Lost Love.* The Traveler's hand. Detail

Lieve Jerger. *The Carriage of Lost Love.* The Traveler. Detail

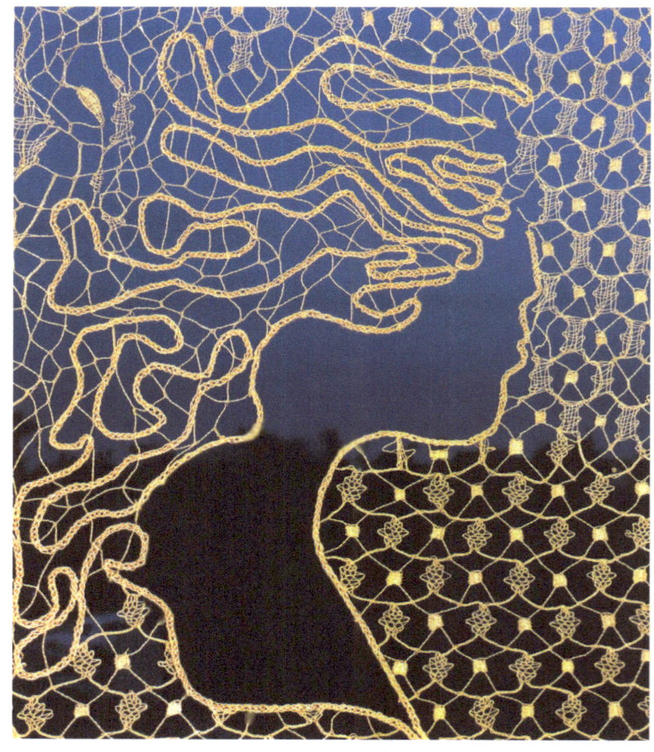

## Nava Lubelski

Raised in New York, Nava Lubelski incorporates the chaos, randomness, aggression, awkwardness, impatience, and beauty of that city in her lace forms. She began to experiment with lace as an outgrowth of her embroidery work. She had been creating embroidered "paintings" on canvas. As her work evolved, she began to cut holes in the canvas and use lace-like stitching to hold the canvas together, playing around with decorative qualities in the stitching. As her work moved more in the direction of sculpture, she taught herself needle lace from a library book. Briefly she considered bobbin lace but thought it "too removed from the hand", concluding that needle lace felt like it had more improvisational possibilities.

Lubelski's work focuses on the contradictions and commonalities between the impulse to destroy and the compulsion to mend, juxtaposing acts of aggression such as spilling, shredding and cutting with restorative labor and reconstruction. She often uses snippets of old lace which she "repairs" and grows into larger pieces.

*[a cast of my left hand in the shape of a] Glove, v. 2* was produced as part of a series of hand casts that earned the artist finalist status in the *Love Lace* competition held by the Powerhouse Museum in Sydney, Australia in 2011.[43] In these, using her left hand as a mold, she stitches only with the right hand. The stitching is expressionistic and improvisational eschewing traditional needle lace precepts of tensioning and regularity while wedding found objects, often crochet, in a disorderly matrix of openwork.

*[a cast of my left hand in the shape of a] Glove (v. 1-5)* is a series of hands molded with one hand as the model, while the other constructs the piece. The found threads and trimmings are leftovers from forgotten or discarded collections, most found on ebay as adult children sell off the carefully hoarded remnants from a dead mother's sewing collection. The resulting hand casts are copies of living flesh, but the fragile, ghostly forms acknowledge the past. The difficulty of the one-handed process results in lace-like creations that are simultaneously delicate and clumsy, both intricately Victorian and roughly modern.

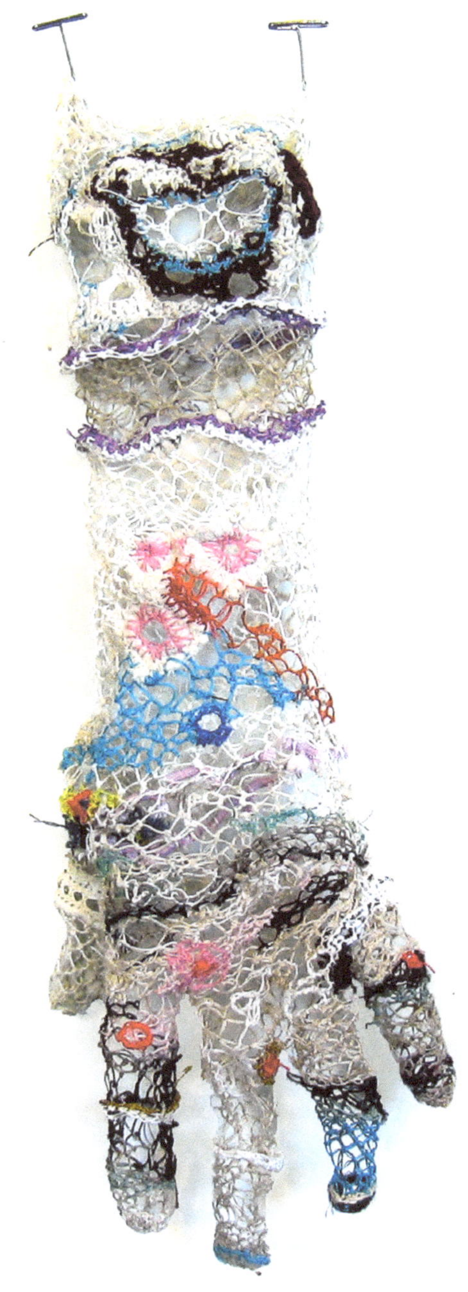

Nava Lubelski. *[a cast of my left hand in the shape of a] Glove v. 2,* 2008. Needle lace, thread and found trimmings, 10″ x 5″ x 2″. Photo: Nava Lubelski.

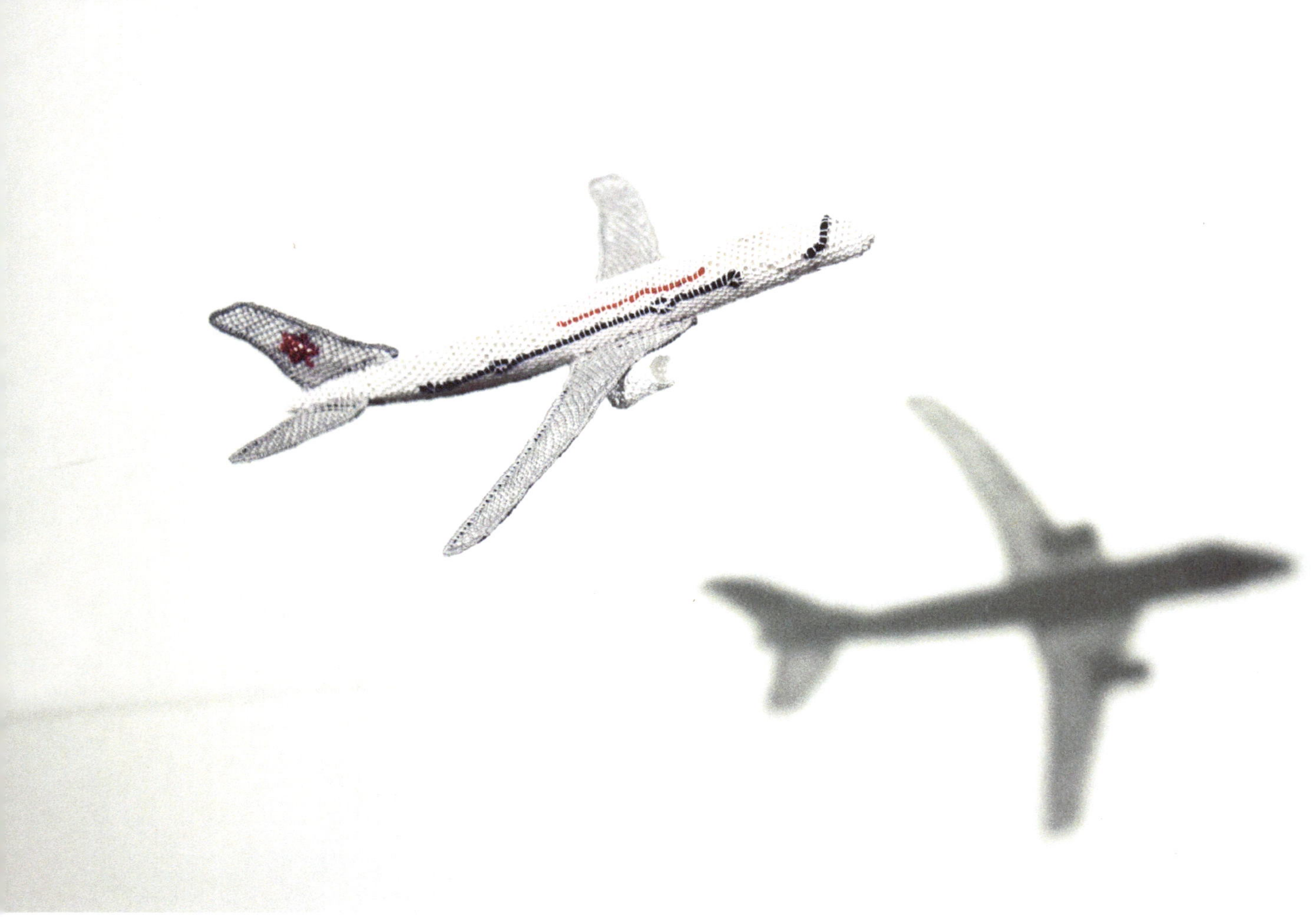

## Dorie Millerson

Dorie Millerson creates small sculptures and installations using needle lace technique and colored sewing thread. Her work deals with attachments between people and things, often symbolized by transportation. Shadow play creates a fluctuating sense of scale in which her toy sized sculptures cast oversized shadows in a world of changing perspectives.[44]

Millerson was originally trained in illustration and weaving. Interested in creating narratives in her work, needle lace gave her the ability to create an organic structure that mirrored her drawings as it is not confined to a woven grid. She began to work in lace during her master's studies at Nova Scotia College of Art and Design teaching herself from Valerie Grimwood's *Starting Needle Lace: A Course for Beginners* [45] borrowed from the public library.

In her master's research, Millerson considered lace as a symbol of time passing describing it as a "time based" medium. She believes that the slow repetitive nature of construction influences the experience of making the work, encouraging contemplation. The intimate nature of the work connects her to the forms she makes in that she touches every thread to create the form. It is meaningful to her to be engaged with the material in this way.

Millerson's work is conducted in a uniformly spaced corded buttonhole stitch. She relies on color, not variation of stitch, to define areas. When Millerson wants to create a thin line, such as the stripes on *Taxicab*, she uses a contrasting colored thread for the cording. Her buttonhole stitches which are generously spaced, as in *point de gaze*[46], expose the corded thread creating a well-defined line. Millerson's process starts with studying a structure and making drawings and paper models to figure out how to make the form and which colors to use. Once she has the form developed she draws each piece as a flat pattern on fabric and creates the lace structure on top. In needle lace it is possible to make a finished shape with a very complex outline. That is, it is unnecessary to hem or secure the edges in any way. So, Millerson can make very intricate structures crafted from precisely shaped

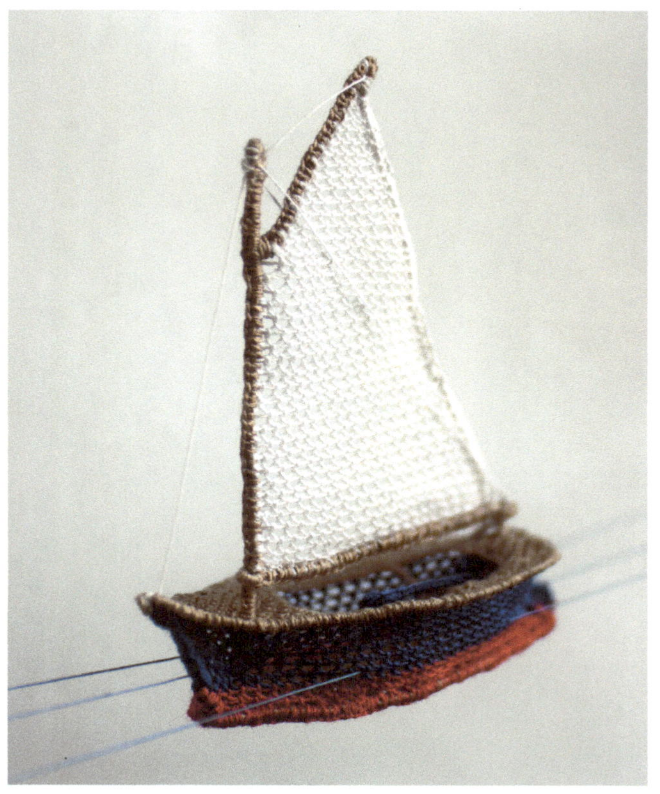

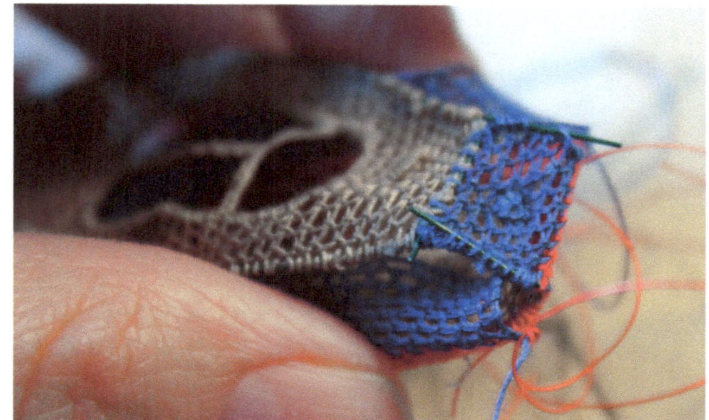

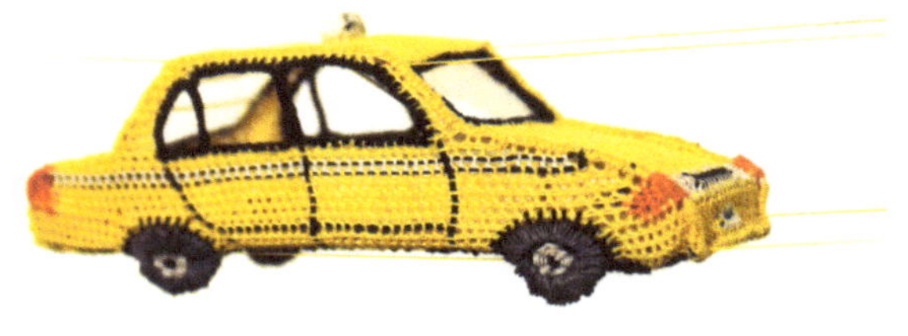

flat pieces. After she has removed the lace pieces from the fabric pattern she joins them in three-dimensional structures with finishing stitching resembling cordonnette. Since some of her structures are stuffed, her stitching de-emphasizes transparency.

The artist was kind enough to create a work specifically for this show. *The Catboat* is a sailboat historically associated with New Jersey. It was initially a work boat used on the shore. As New Jersey became a vacation area for visitors from New York and Philadelphia, the catboat was developed for racing and recreation. As such it is deeply resonant to a state whose shore has been a source of economic prosperity, both in food production and in tourism.

The three pieces are part of an ongoing series of works that investigates memory, distance and attachments to people, places, and possessions. Each time I make a new piece, I learn something new about how we build our structures and what they mean. Working on *Catboat* allowed me to start to consider how and why these small boats are built, who builds them and who sails in them.

Dorie Millerson. *Airplane*, 2011. Needle lace, cotton, wire, acetate, 1.5″ x 5.25″ x 5″. Photo: Dorie Millerson.

Dorie Millerson. *Catboat*, 2018. Needle lace, cotton, wire, 2.75″ x 2.75″ x 1.18″. Photo: Dorie Millerson

Dorie Millerson. *Catboat*. Process.

Dorie Millerson. *Taxicab*, 2011. Needle lace, cotton, wire, acetate, 1.25″ x 3.1″ x 1″. Photo: Dorie Millerson.

## Penny Nickels

A fourth-generation artist living in the Pacific Northwest, Penny Nickels' work explores myths, storytelling, and archetypes. Although she works in fiber art, her background is in printmaking. She has participated in group shows in the U.S. and U.K. and has written extensively on contemporary and traditional needlework for *mrxstitch.com*, an online site that explores contemporary embroidery and needlecraft.

Nickels became interested in lace in about 2010 while studying Tudor era portraits for an article about blackwork embroidery. Conceiving that lace might be a medium suited to her artistic practice she educated herself using books that had been scanned into free online libraries. Many of these books were from the *Digital Archive of Documents Related to Lace.*[47] Nickels cites the following books as her sources, some from the 17th century, and some from the late 19th century. *Corona delle nobili et virtuose donne by Cesare Vecellio* (1592), *Les Singuliers et Nouveaux Pourtraicts* by Federico de Vinciolo (1587), *Encyclopedia of Needlework* by Thérèse de Dillmont (1886), *Lace, Ancient and Modern: Comprising a History of Its Origin and Manufacture, with Instructions Concerning the Manner of Making it* by Mrs. C. D. Beebe (1880), *Point and Pillow Lace: a short account of various kinds ancient and modern, and how to recognize them* by Mary Sharp (1899), *Chats on Old Lace and Needlework* by Mrs Lowes (1908), and various *Home Needlework Magazines* from the late 1800's to the early 1900's.

Of her choice to work in needle lace technique, Nickels says:

*I've found lace to be an especially rewarding medium because of the dynamism inherent in the working of it, the contradictions it contains. It's both strong and fragile, opulent and simple. It's a risky medium. It's difficult to tell what the piece will look like until it's complete because of the way it's constructed. My pieces generally take between 10 and 18 months, and I've found spending that much time with a subject forces me to explore it deeply. I'm always surprised by what I discover.*

Penny Nickels. *The Jersey Devil,* 2016. Needle lace, 15″ x 20″. Photo: Penny Nickels.

Nickels' lace artistry is highly informed by her history as a printmaker. Like printmaking, lacework is largely a monochrome art form where the design is achieved through pattern and texture. In *Just Girly Things* the illusion of three-dimensionality is created on the scorpion pincers by varying the density of the buttonhole stitch to create the appearance of reflected light. The sky behind *The Jersey Devil* is the stitching equivalent of cross hatching.

In *The Jersey Devil* Nickels employs a wide range of buttonhole stitch variations, undoubtedly taken from 19th century lace manuals, to achieve different tonalities in the figures, house, and trees. She also works in different weights of thread. Voided hoof prints, the signature of the Jersey Devil, appear in a landscape that transitions from fine snow to gritty sand. The different terrains are achieved by working the same stitch, corded buttonhole stitch, with different weights of thread starting with the lightest on the left-hand side to the coarsest where the sand meets the sea. Devotees of New Jersey folklore will be delighted that *The Jersey Devil* is making its debut in this exhibition in its home state.

In *Just Girly Things*, a reinterpretation of the "Just Girly Things" internet meme, Nickels imports some of the techniques of 17th century Venetian *gros point*, notably in the form of heavily raised padded outlines (cordonet). Here she uses less of a palette of different stitches, relying more on corded buttonhole stitch with "portes" or voided areas. The appearance of perspective is achieved using a distorted "laid grid" stitch. These stitches, in their undistorted form were popular in the *point de gaze* needle laces of the late 19th century. Thus, the artist has used a variety of techniques from different eras to create her own aesthetic.

Most notable about Nickels' work is her choice of subject matter. Perhaps because of its history as a fashion item, lace themes have largely been floral, or geometric. However, as lace transitions from fashion to art, 21st century lacemakers are free to choose darker themes. Nickels' work reflects an aesthetic that rejects superficial decoration embracing themes of witchcraft and the supernatural. Her work exudes a Feminism imbued with atavistic power.

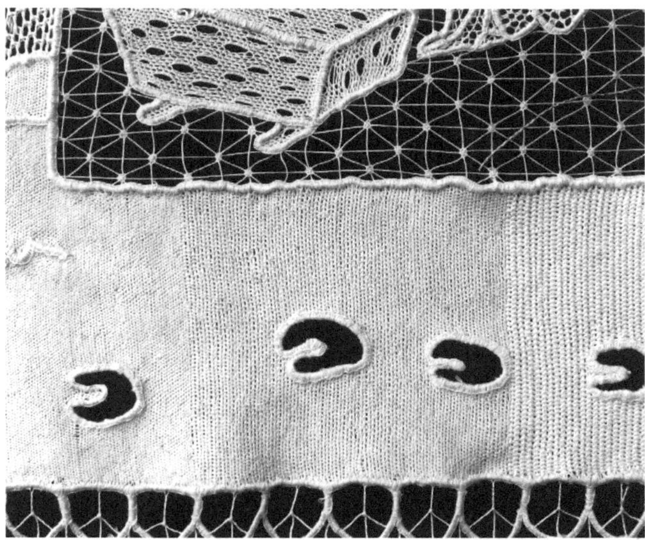

Penny Nickels. *The Jersey Devil.* Detail of textural effects produced by using different thread weights to signify the transition from fine snow to sand.

Key for The Jersey Devil

Each corner: Bell, book, candle, and date. 1735 is the birthdate of The Jersey Devil, the bell, bible, and candle are the instruments a local clergyman used in an attempt to exorcise the Jersey Devil from the Pine Barrens.

Left side: Commodore Stephen Decatur in front of a stand of pines, fires a cannonball at the Jersey Devil, but the Devil is unharmed.

Center: Jane Leeds. Legend has it that in 1735, Mother Leeds already had twelve children. After becoming pregnant for the thirteenth time, she cursed the child in frustration and said the child would be the devil, or in some accounts, offered the child to the devil.

Upper right-hand side: The Jersey Devil facing off against Stephen Decatur

Bottom left: Mermaid covering her face in fear at the cannon explosion. The Jersey Devil is interesting because it's one of the few monsters that apparently enjoys the company of other monsters. Some legends say he enjoyed laughing at shipwrecks with mermaids.

Bottom: Hoof prints in the snow. In 1901 several sightings of the Jersey Devil were reported, hoof prints in the snow offered as proof.

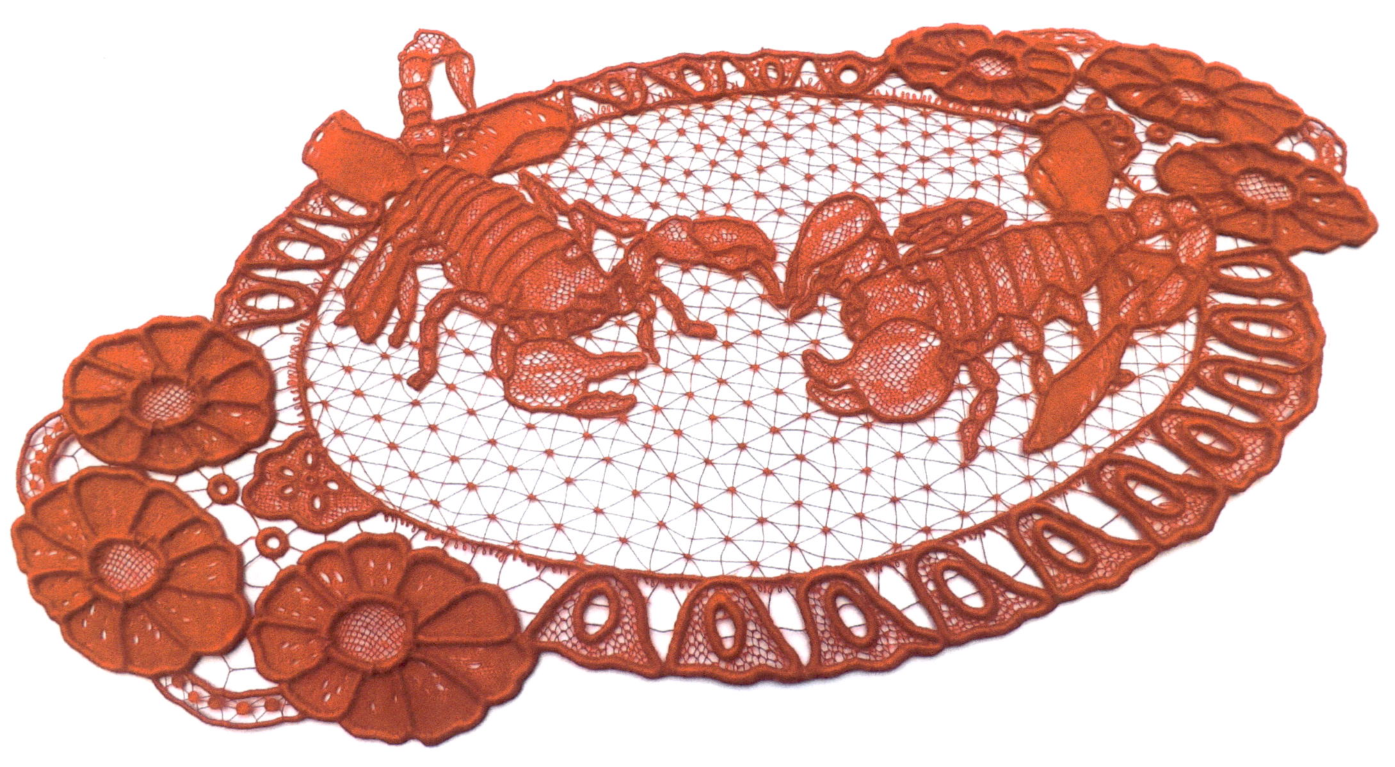

Penny Nickels. *Just Girly Things*, 2017. Handmade lace, 7″ x 15″. Photo: Penny Nickels

No matter what medium I'm working in, I enjoy exploring mythology and liminal spaces. My work is generally an interpretation of those stories and spaces. I especially like lace because I find it to be meaningful in multilayered ways, which allows me to examine ideas with fresh eyes and reach conclusions that surprise me.

I chose to work in lace for *The Jersey Devil* because I thought it reflected the historical period well, while conveying a sense of interconnectedness, the story's "thread" that runs through over two hundred years of sightings and folklore about the monster.

In *Just Girly Things* there's the obvious use of lace to reinforce a sense of florid femininity that the phrase "girly things" invokes, while the composition is more about divination (entomomancy) and animal-baiting as entertainment. Thread doing double duty here as a nod to fate deities such as the Moirai and the Norns, while also acknowledging the history of fancy needlework being considered an appropriate pastime for girls.

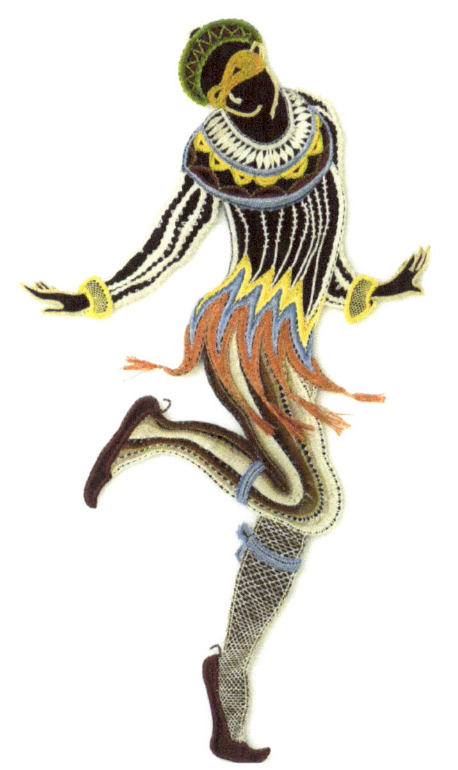

## Wako Ono

Wako Ono is a graduate of Joshibi University of Art and Design where she studied Japanese painting. In 1988 she encountered lacemaking in an adult school in London. She was fascinated with it and studied Honiton and other traditional British laces with the well-renowned teacher Margaret Susans. She has also studied with Pamela Nottingham, Ulrike Voelcker and Sandi Woods.

Ono enjoys using various traditional lace techniques while making original lace work based on her own designs. She says she "dares" to use kimono inspired colored threads, but also unique materials such as metal and plastics as in other modern arts. She has had four solo exhibitions of her lace work in Tokyo.

Although bobbin lace is considered a European craft tradition, there was a government sponsored school teaching Honiton lace in Yokohama as early as 1885.[48] Ono believes that there are synchronies between lacemaking and traditional Japanese handicrafts and notes that many Japanese lacemakers are well versed in other skill intensive crafts. It is her opinion that the Japanese find lace to be enchanting because of its beauty and delicacy.

She explains her passion for lace in this way:

*"Lace" is commonly regarded as a mere textile, however, I believe that "Lace" can be a way of expressing our thoughts, impressions, and passion as like paintings. In that sense, I feel some similarity between "Lace" and the traditional Japanese Painting which I majored in at an art university in Tokyo. The former consists of lines (threads), and the latter of dots (powdered mineral pigments). The fusion of tradition and expression is very challenging, but worth tackling as my lifework. And in addition, it is great "fun"!*

In *Joy*, one of a series of Harlequins made for Ono's most recent Tokyo exhibition, the artist uses the part lace technique of Honiton. In Honiton one is able to weave free standing and connected shapes without a background mesh. Named after the market town in England in the center of the Devonshire lacemaking regions, Honiton was a very popular technique for weaving naturalistic flowers in the 19th century. These flowers would be collected by intermediaries and taken to a workshop where they would be joined into such items as collars or handkerchief edgings.[49] Ono also demonstrates a very clear debt to Sandi Woods in her use of gradations of color, side by side, in cloth stitch. Sandi Woods introduced this "painterly" use of color in a series of breathtaking books which transformed traditional Milanese tape lace into kaleidoscopic orgies of color play.[50] Milanese tape is a lace in which pins are used only at the edges of decorative braids. The interior flow of threads is capable of tremendous variety and geometric intricacy, which is emphasized in Woods' work by establishing different colors for the different paths of threads. Ono eschews the more complicated interior color plays in favor of using subtle gradations of color in solid areas to create a very rich tapestry like effect.

I expressed human general feelings through Harlequin.
They were inspired by an Italian Commedia dell' arte.
Often unaware we mask our feelings and play on our life stage.

Wako Ono. *Joy*, 2014. Cotton thread, velvet film, 21″ x 12″.

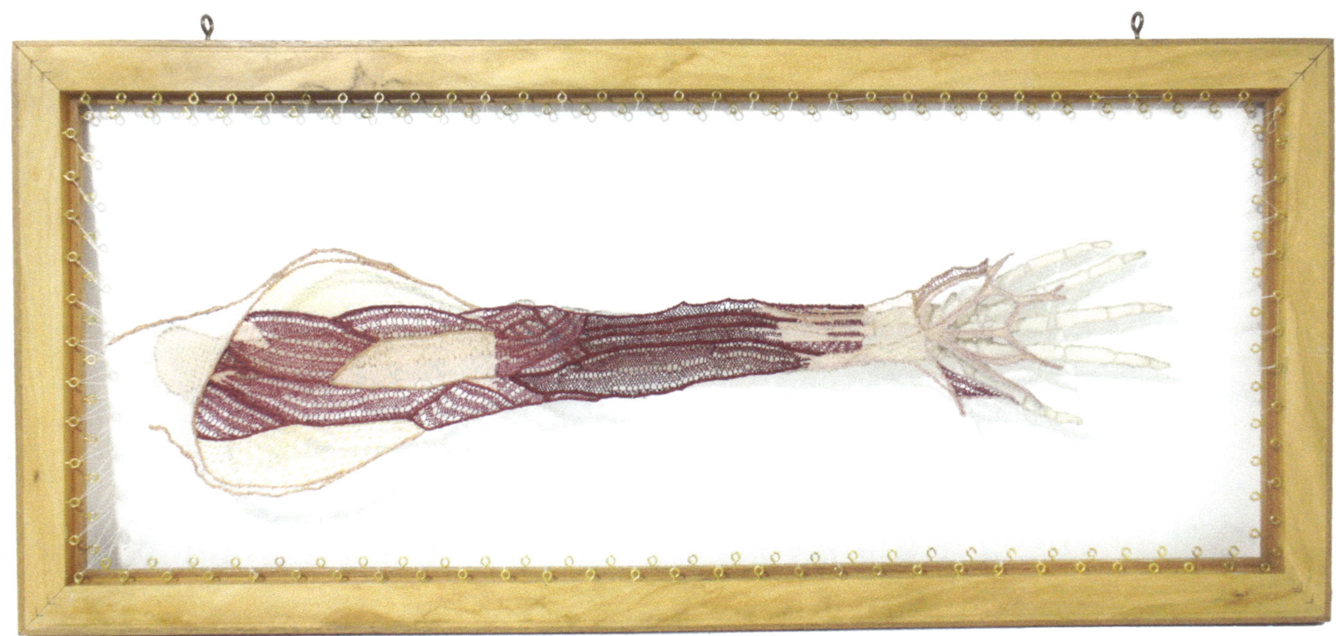

## E.J.Parkes

Perhaps the youngest artist in the show, E.J.Parkes is a student at the Wimbledon College of Art, University of the Arts, London. Parkes credits her interest in lace to an aunt who taught her to tat and also provided some bobbins and a Honiton lace pillow. But, ultimately, Parkes chose to work in needle lace which she taught herself.

Parkes is a disabled textile artist. She began to learn lace after she had suffered a relapse causing her to leave her studies at the Birmingham Metropolitan College. She finds that the medium of needle lace is well suited to a life in which physical movement is constrained. Lace work, which is traditionally small, but very intricate provides the perfect outlet for her creative energy. She often works from bed or the sofa when she is too ill to go out. She is inspired by historic and contemporary lace and embroidery, as well as the natural world, biology, and anatomy. Currently she is focused on exploring the intersections in fragility between the human body and lace.

*Anterior Aspect* is one of Parkes' larger works, taking 250 hours to complete. The work is mounted so that it can be seen from both sides. The obverse of the work reveals the underlying bone rendered entirely in solid corded buttonhole stitch. Some larger stitching at the finger joints creates the appearance of a gap that mimics an image on an x-ray. The front, or "anterior aspect", shows the muscles, fascia and connective tissue rendered in a multiplicity of needle lace stitches. The effect of striations in the red muscle tissue is cleverly delineated in negative space achieved with varying stitch size and spacing. Lace work has traditionally exploited transparency in all possible gradations. Parkes has exploited this feature of lace work in that the bone is selectively revealed from the anterior aspect by the different transparencies of the stitching of the different categories of soft tissue. Sensing a similarity between lace work and anatomical illustrations with three-dimensional effects and cut outs, Parkes has employed a medium that obscures and reveals in realizing her work.

My first love was biology; my obsession with anatomy, zoology and the natural sciences has continued, and my work is mainly based around exploring these themes. For this piece I was interested in how I can use the flexibility of different lace making techniques, as well as 3D elements to examine the fragility and complexity that lace and the human body share. Those similarities are what I hoped to navigate here.

E.J.Parkes. *Anterior Aspect,* 2015. Needle lace, 37.2″ x 16.2″ x 2″. Photo: E.J. Parkes.

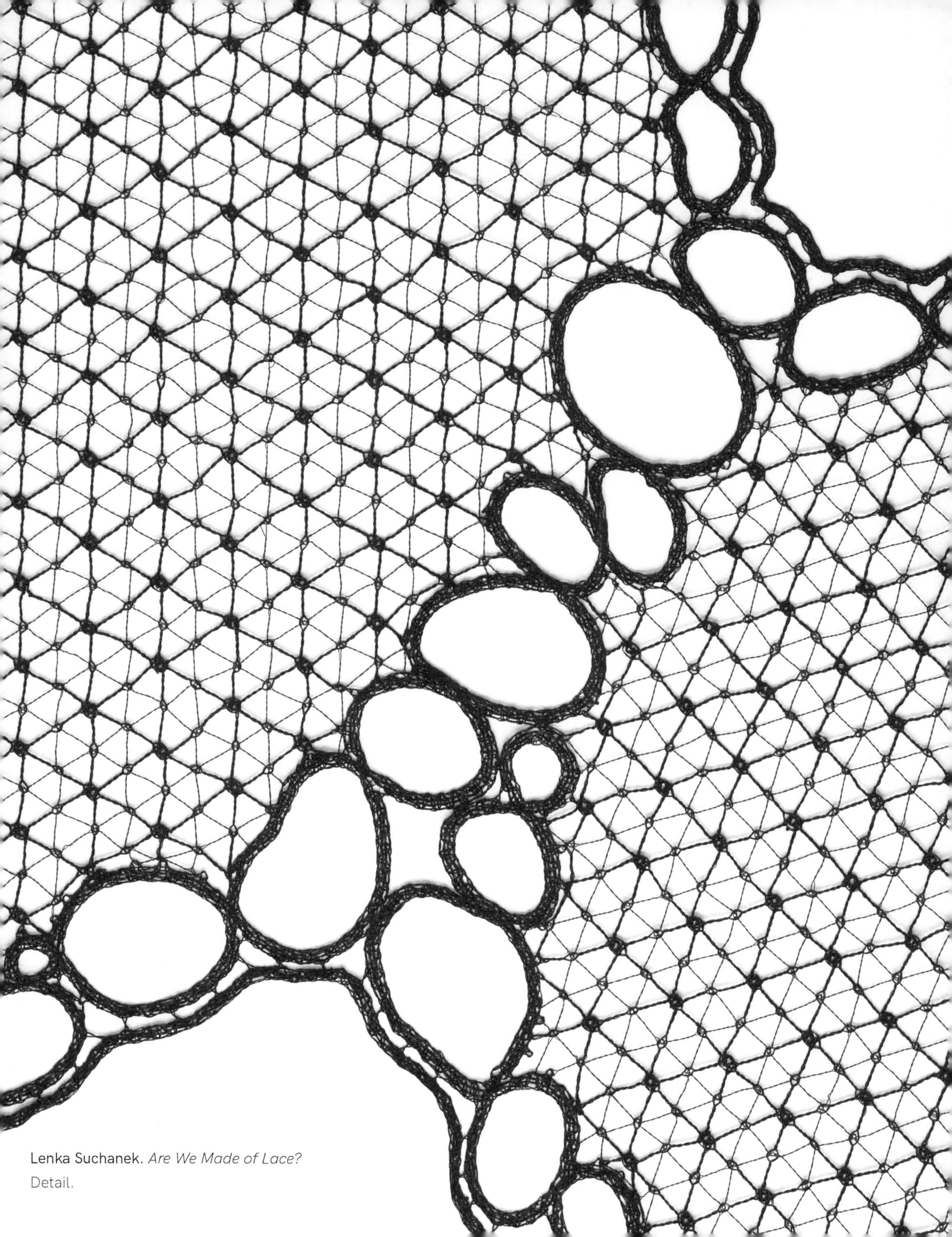

Lenka Suchanek. *Are We Made of Lace?*
Detail.

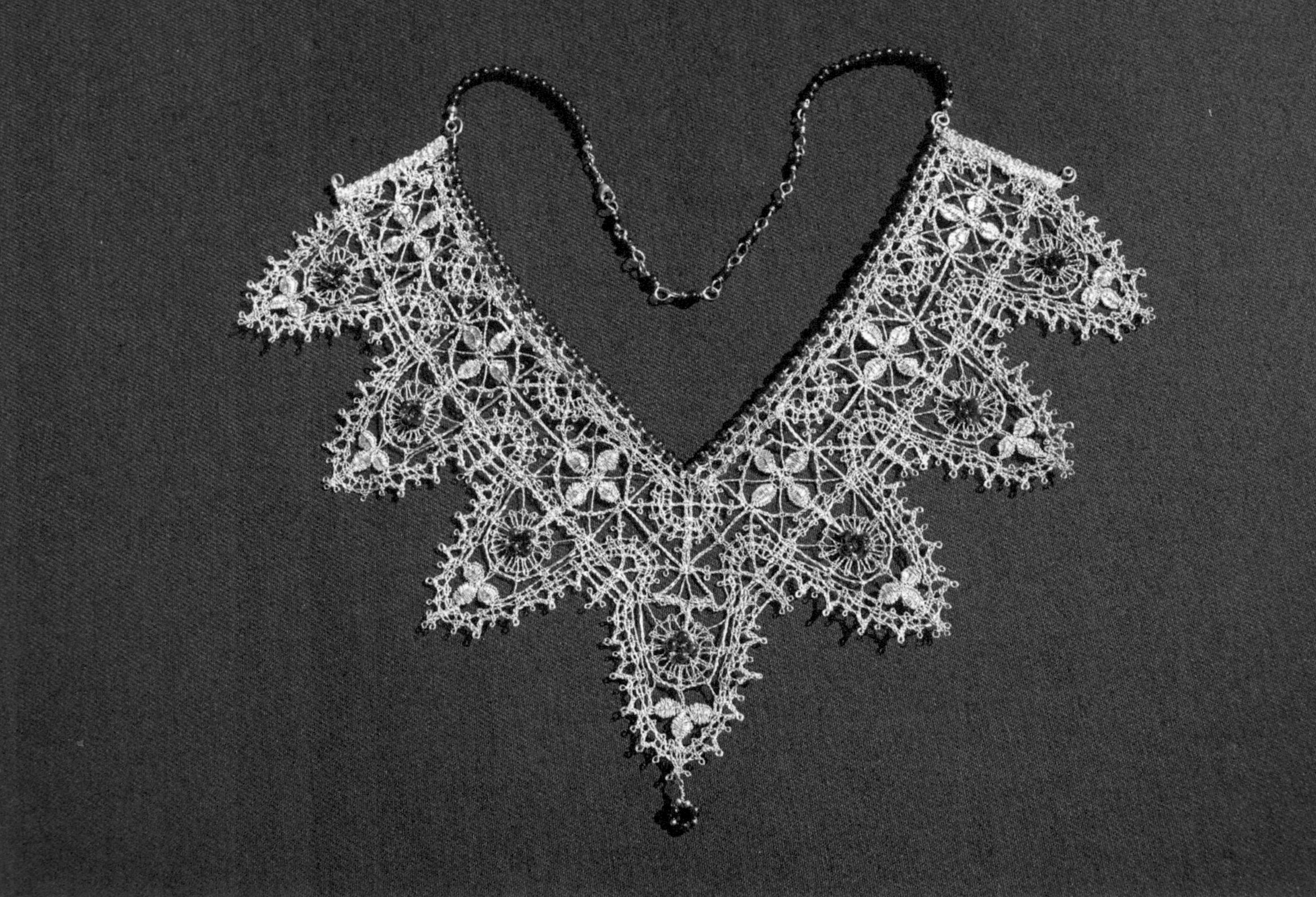

## Lenka Suchanek

A major figure in contemporary lace, Lenka Suchanek was raised in Czechoslovakia before moving to Canada, a country without a lacemaking tradition, twenty-five years ago. She realized that fiber lace was not a good fit for the Canadian West Coast lifestyle. Considering alternatives, she discovered that copper wire could be used instead of thread if the tools and techniques were adapted. Curiosity to expand and experiment led her to make lace art in a wide range of styles and subject matter. Always open to new ideas, Suchanek has even begun to incorporate the mathematically derived grounds of Veronika Irvine in some small lace "sketches".

While still in Czechoslovakia, Suchanek taught herself the basic bobbin lace stitches from a magazine before becoming fascinated with Elena Holeczyova. Holeczyova was one of the first Czech/Slovak lace designers to transform lace craft into art. After graduating from the School of Fine Arts and Crafts in Prague in 1926 Holeczykova worked with lacemakers in the Slovak countryside, incorporating traditional lace techniques in her original, modern, large scale works. She was a major inspiration for the modern lace art movement in Czechoslovakia in the 1960s and 1970s which influenced Suchanek. Suchanek believes that the evolution of Czech lace from craft to art form is deeply rooted in the Czech National Revival movement of the late 18th and 19th centuries which looked to the folk-art tradition preserved in the Czech countryside to create an identity after years of being politically dominated by other cultures.

In *Genoese Scallop Necklace* Suchanek drew on period portrait paintings, antique lace examples and historic pattern books to design a wide scalloped lace in the style of the standing and falling collars popular in the European courts of the late Renaissance and early Baroque period. Genoese lace is characterized by a geometric appearance, and leaf shaped tallies are considered a defining feature. When executed in silver wire, as Suchanek has done, the petal shaped tallies reflect the light very opulently, making a breathtaking modern necklace.

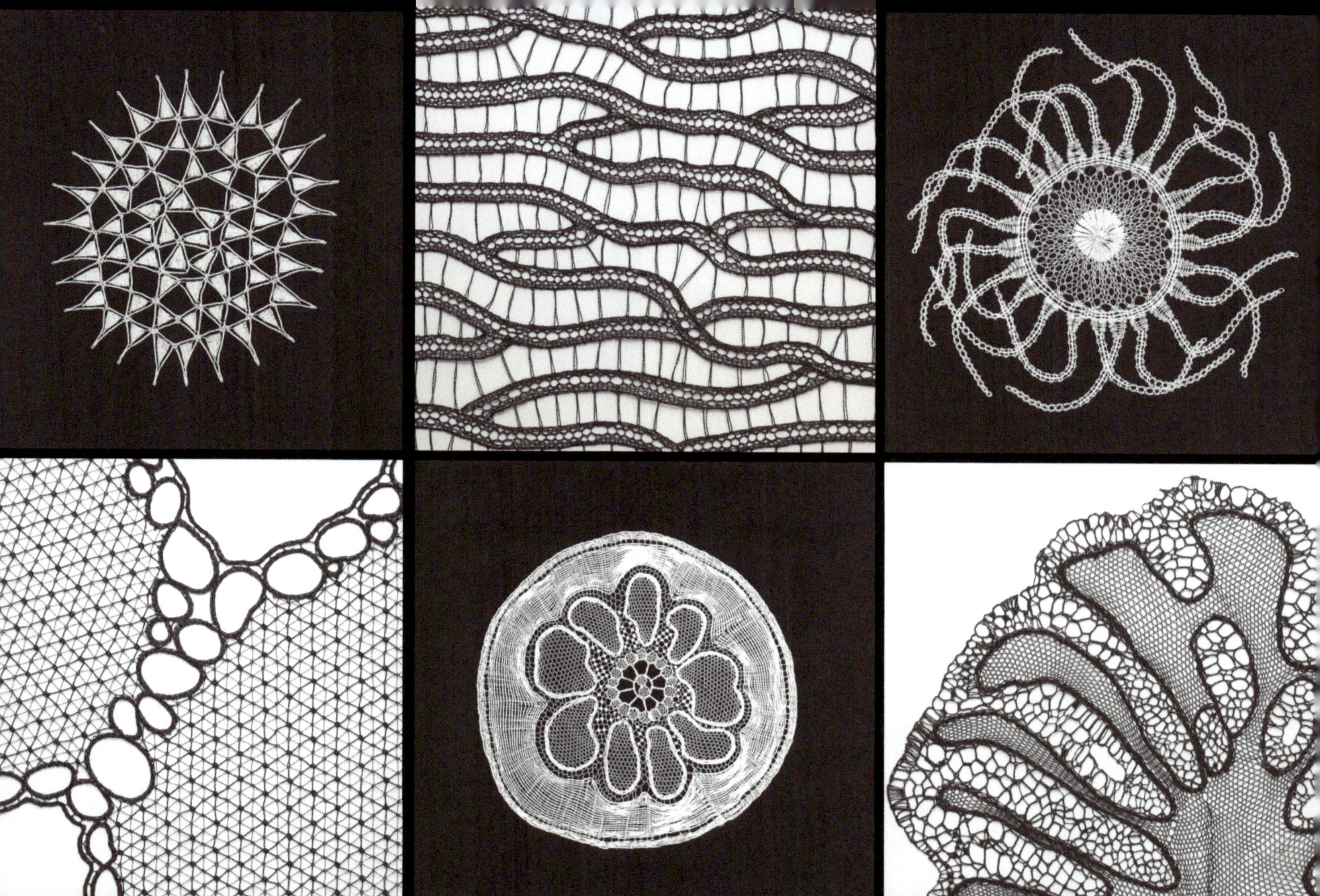

Suchanek's other piece, *Are We Made of Lace?*, is inspired by electron microscope scans of cells. In this piece the artist combines a wide amalgam of lace techniques derived from different lace traditions showing her consummate mastery of lace and her ability to employ whatever technique fits the purpose without regard to any one lace discipline. There are triangular tallies characteristic of guipure laces. There are complex snowflake based grounds which are associated with Flemish laces. There are tapes connected with long sewings which are a Czech contemporary tape lace specialty. Square tallies and the use of gimp in the middle cell of the bottom row reference English point ground laces. The cell on the lower right side is a half stitch area surrounded by a lace structure composed of plaiting, tallies, ten-stick, and multi-pair intersections that are a masterpiece of technical virtuosity in service of a very random looking pattern. Made for the *Love Lace*[51] competition, this piece won Suchanek finalist status.

Lenka Suchanek. *Genoese Scallop Necklace*, 2001. Silver wire, garnets, 10.6″ x 7″. [opposite page]

Lenka Suchanek. *Are We Made of Lace?*, 2012. Enameled copper on acrylic background, metal frames, handmade bobbin lace techniques, 30″ x 45″. Photo: Peter Flynn Niznansky.

I have always wondered what is so unique about lacemaking process and why it facilitates connection with our inner nature. Is it a result of focused activity and deep concentration? Shared knowledge passed on through generations? Or something else?

When I came across scanning electron microscope images of organic tissues, it felt like finding the missing piece of the puzzle. The close-up pictures of cell ensembles look exactly like lace. Everything - plants, sea plankton, humans - is made from a primordial lace that cannot be seen with the unaided eye, but pervades all living forms.

I found the answer to my question. We are part of an awesome lace world and making lace by hand is uncovering the fundamental blueprint of life.

## Lauran Sundin

Lauran Sundin constructs sensuous and sculptural body adornment in precious wire using bobbin lace technique. Sundin's families' roots in England and Scotland created a reverence for the traditional fiber crafts of the British Isles. Born in Rhode Island, in which machine lacemaking was once a major industry, her early childhood in history-rich New England cemented an interest in the past. Teenage years in California exposed her to contemporary design and Japanese-style open-plan living, which led her to explore Japanese culture. She studied Japanese textiles, especially weaving, at the University of Hawaii. As a weaver she found that she was artistically pushing the boundaries of loom weaving, only to discover that many of the technical solutions she was inventing had already been invented by bobbin lacemakers. Taking to the road via youth hostels, she added traditional bobbin lace techniques to the tool kit she had derived from her experiments in off-loom weaving.

Sundin's wire bobbin lace jewelry has earned her many accolades, from being a finalist in the *Love Lace* competition in Sydney, Australia to inclusion in *Imagine...Lace at Waddesdon*. Durability is a persistent challenge to makers of wire lace jewelry. Sundin has conquered the problem with unique techniques that stabilize and add firmness to her structures. She is also well known for weaving in two planes simultaneously, a form that can be seen in *Typhoon*, where the black and copper colored mesh interweave to create a three-dimensional structure which is perceived by the alternation in color.

*Typhoon* was made for the *Love Lace*[52] competition. The concept underlying the piece is that several necklaces were blown apart in a tropical storm, a typhoon, and then came together to form an entirely new piece.

Lace has served me well: enabling me to achieve my goal of "weaving in any direction" to create innovative sculptural pieces of jewelry.

A piece of lace must fill many roles. First it must function well; i.e., a pillow case or table runner must work well in that capacity. My pieces are to be worn, so I pay great attention to the fit and movement of my jewelry on the human body.

Form must not only follow function, pieces must be pleasing when viewed from any angle. Shapes must be striking when viewed across a room. As a viewer gets closer to the wearer the initial overall shape gives way to motifs which form the whole. At close inspection the details and workmanship are revealed.

The material that a piece is constructed from must be an integral part of what that piece is all about. I combine the qualities of precious metals - ductility, rigidity, the glow of gold - with bits of techniques from many types of lace. To me the finished form is more important than the strict adherence to any particular method. I've explored using black plastic as added support; combined stainless steel wire with pearls; added gemstones to delicate mesh constructions; and developed novel ways to fasten diverse materials together in structurally sound, aesthetically pleasing combinations. I've tested ways of altering springiness and colors of metals, and wrangled computer programs into giving me contemporary versions of traditional lace designs. Since so few people have tried what I am doing, the challenge of experimentation and solving problems has become part of the fun.

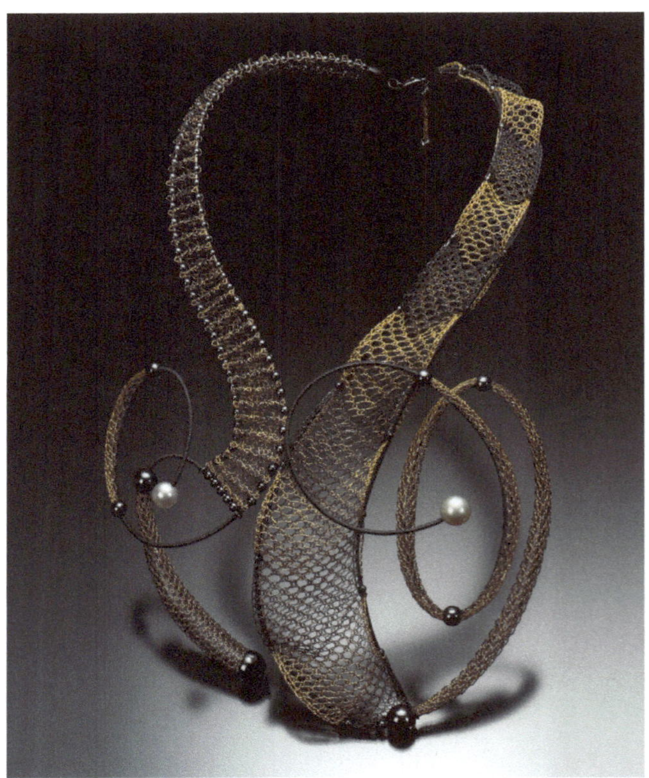

Lauran Sundin. *Typhoon*, 2011. 14 and 18 karat gold with oxidized sterling silver wire, Tahitian pearls, vinyl, bobbin lace technique, 18″ x 9″. Photo: Brelian Arts.

## Olivia Valentine

There was a great deal of excitement in the lace community when Olivia Valentine was awarded a Fulbright Fellowship. It was widely seen as an acknowledgment of the medium. Valentine's interest in lacemaking began in graduate school where research in openwork led her to a study of lace structures. She was excited by bobbin lace because it is a textile that has a very direct relationship to drawing. One may draw the design and make the lace on the drawing.

Valentine is self-taught. Starting with a kit from the iconic lace supply store Lacis, she relied on Geraldine Stott's *The Bobbin Lace Manual*[53] in her learning process. While attending the *Doily Free Zone: Young Lacemakers Symposium* in 2013[54] she met Mariña Regueiro, a Spanish lace teacher, who was to be influential on her work.

Valentine has combined her background as an architect and her skill as a photographer with lacemaking. Her entry to the *Love Lace* competition in 2011 was an architecturally inspired window construction called *Punto in Aria*.[55] *Punto in aria*, meaning stitches in the air, is a form of needle lace in which lacemakers of the 16th century broke free of the fabric-based structure of cutwork allowing for greater design freedom. Valentine is making a little joke in her title. Her work is not made in *punto in aria* technique. It is made in Torchon bobbin lace. The term "stitches in the air" in this piece signifies that it appears to be suspended from helium filled mylar balloons in a nod to Andy Warhol.

In 2012 Valentine combined the Fulbright Fellowship and the Brandford/Elliott Award for Excellence in Fiber Art[56] to travel in Turkey studying Oya, a traditional lace of Anatolia which resulted in two works. *Panorama*, is an architectural scale Oya made of balcony tarp and incorporating a landscape of mountains (traditional) with motifs representing the modern international style apartment blocks of the city scape of Izmar. The other piece, *Walking Oya*, is a photographic work in which Valentine herself appears as an Oya motif inserted in the landscape of a small village in Cappadocia. Recently Valentine has been experimenting with lace in performance art.[57]

*The entering takes away* is a large scale minimalist work in Torchon lace which recalls Valentine's background in architecture.

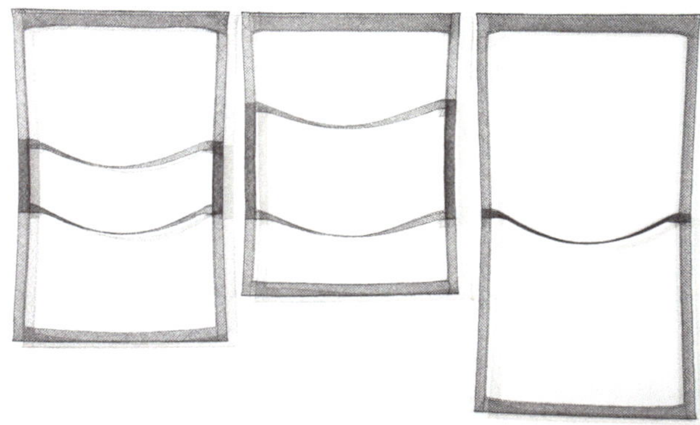

My work as an artist is focused on the construction of edges and interstitial spaces. This line of inquiry began with my investigations into the space of the textile edge. Beginning with early examples of openwork embroidery, I traced the transition of lace structures from the center of a cloth to its edge. I use the window as a literal and metaphorical threshold between interior and exterior space in several of my studio projects, including *The entering takes away*. Lace is often used as an edging, defining the boundaries between the private body and the public world. Windows similarly mediate between interior domestic space and the exterior public world. By constructing windows using the techniques of fabric edging, the threshold between interior and exterior space is expanded.

*Nor was I hungry; so I found*
*That hunger was a way*
*Of persons outside windows,*
*The entering takes away.*

*Emily Dickinson*

Olivia Valentine. *The entering takes away,* 2016. Handwoven linen bobbin lace, steel rods, 54″ x 94″. Photo: Olivia Valentine.

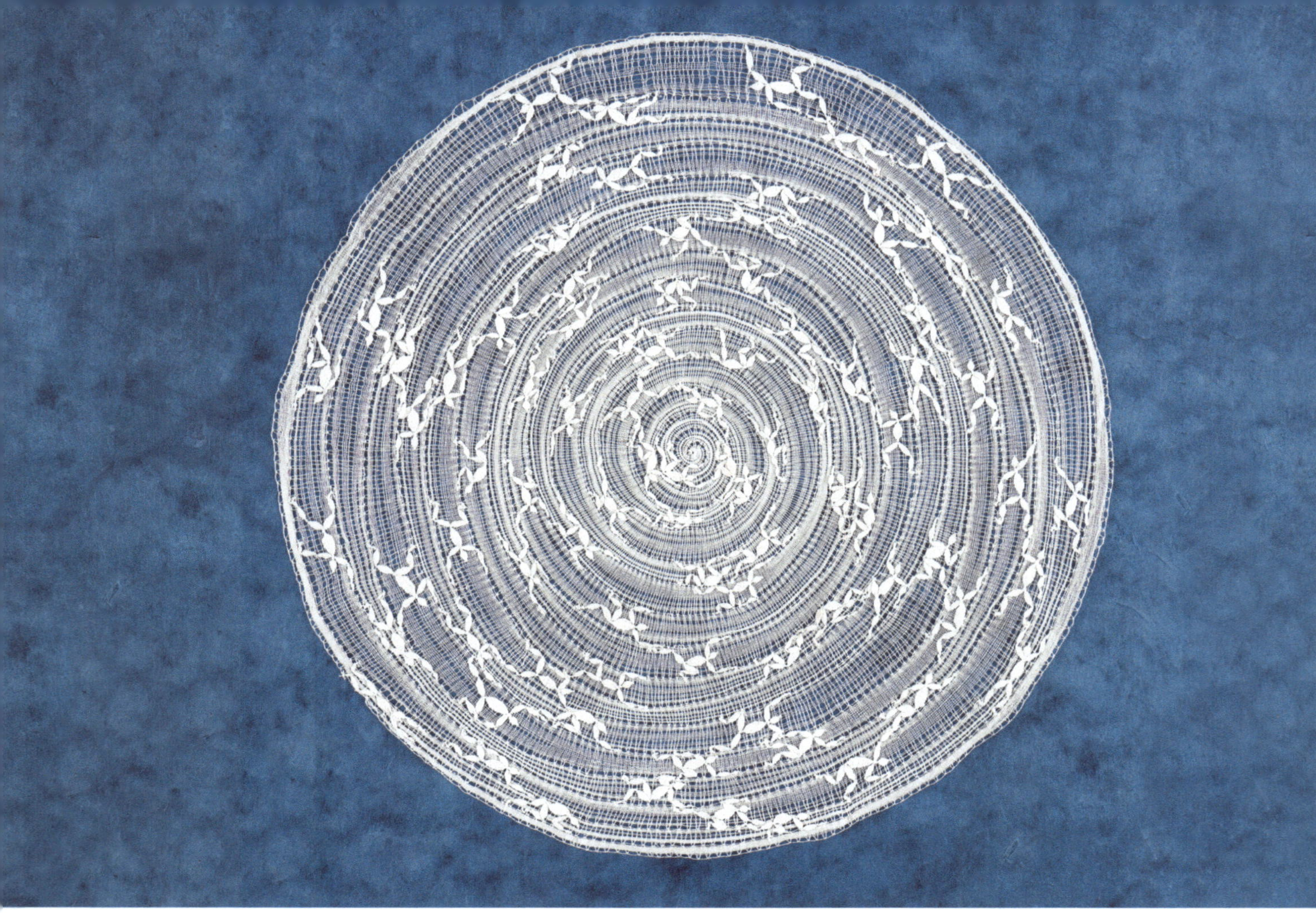

## Nicole Valsesia-Lair

French artist, Nicole Valsesia-Lair found her preferred medium, lace, at the studio of renowned lace artist Françoise Micoud in 1999. Valsesia-Lair was already a fiber artist, having studied at the school of Applied Arts in Duperré, followed by the École Boulle in Paris. In 1978 she studied tapestry at the Manufacture Nationale des Gobelins in Paris. She has exhibited widely in France, Italy and Eastern Europe, winning a first prize in the International Bobbin Lace Competition in Idrija, Slovenia in 2007.

Valsesia-Lair's work often features small anthropomorphic figures made of tallies. The tally is a bobbin lace structure, square, rectangular, or leaf-shaped produced with two pairs.[58] One thread is woven back and forth across the other three. This is an example of single weft weaving, whereas most lace structures consist of double weft weaving. When a lacemaker makes a tally, she can control the width of the tally by careful tensioning of the passive threads. Valsesia-Lair uses large fat tallies for the bodies of her figures, small tallies for the heads, and elongated tallies to realize the arms and legs. An appearance of lithe athleticism is created with leaf shaped tallies forming the limbs, connected as if by joints. In her work, the tally made figures are fashioned in a surprising variety of positions, a tour de force in lace figure study carried out with the most elemental structure of bobbin lace.

In her other works such as *Au pas, au trot, au galop* (walking, trotting, galloping) the tiny figures assume all the postures of human ambulation. In *Petite Boites* they are shown trying to escape from small boxes. In *Dendrovortex* they are sucked helplessly, flailing and struggling into the center of a spiral. The spiral is the cross section of a tree that might be used in the science of Dendrochronology, the study of historical conditions based on tree rings.

*Dendrovortex* was created for a competition whose theme was "Wood". I like this spiral that attracts my little characters in its movement. Are we not sucked in the same way by life? What is there on the other side?

Nicole Valsesia-Lair. *Dendrovortex*, 2012. Bobbin lace, 15″ in diameter. Photo: Atelier 80.

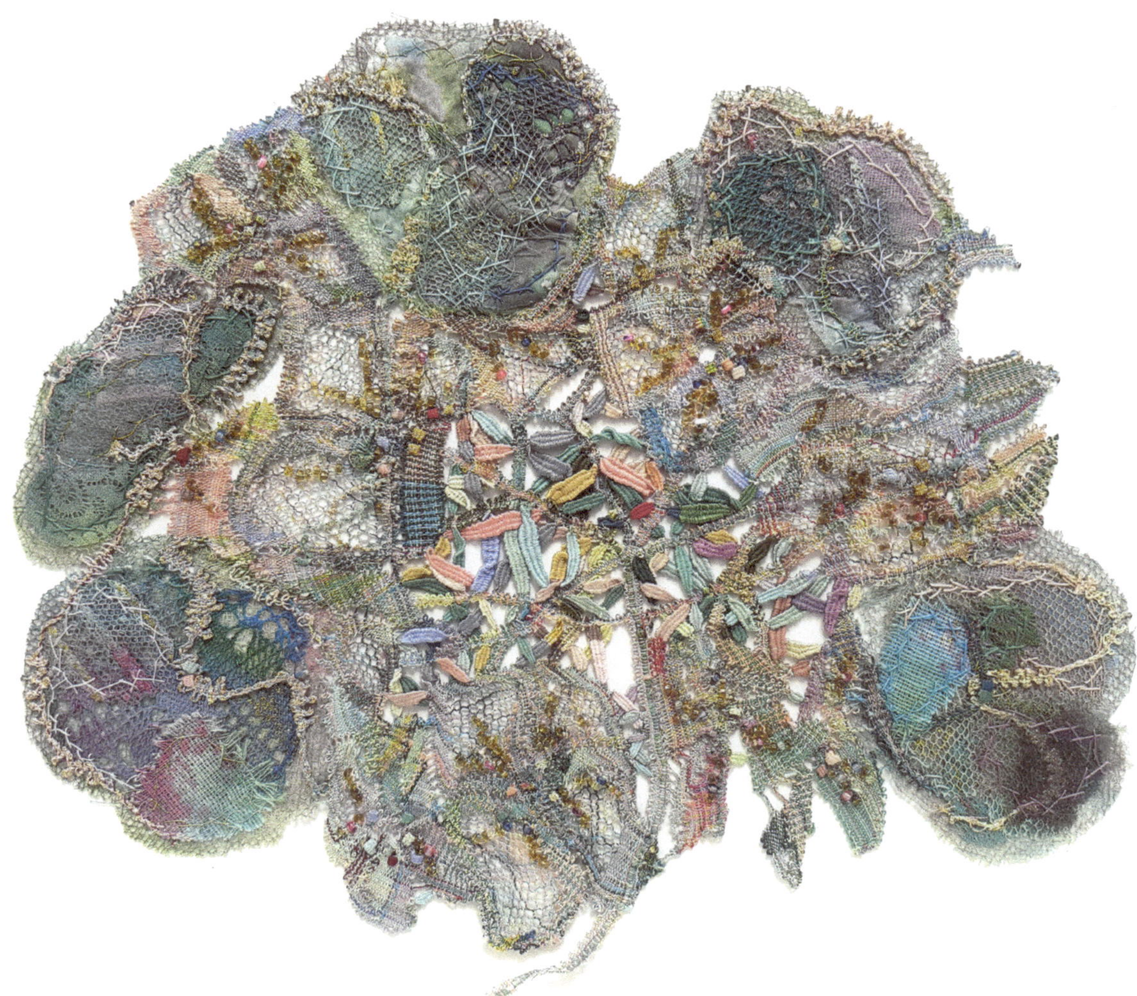

## Denise Watts

"Making bobbin lace wasn't like learning something for the first time, it was like being reminded of something forgotten," Denise Watts says of her first encounter with bobbin lace. Starting with bobbin lace in 1979, Watts is a major figure of the English lace revival. Her work has moved through many phases in that time. *Dried Hydrangea* dates from 1988 and is an exploration of color, texture, and innovation.

Watt's first bobbin lace class was an evening class in traditional lace at an English adult school. She caught on quickly, having an intuitive understanding of bobbin lace structures and by the time the teacher told her she had no more to teach her, Watts had been creating her own designs in secret.

Watts was a 1984 graduate of the City and Guilds Creative Textiles certification, a very rigorous and prestigious qualification. She went on to be part of the first class, called "the guinea pigs", of a City and Guilds qualification program specifically for lacemaking. She has been a lace teacher and an assessor for The Lace Guild's certification programs. She is one of the founding members of the *98 Lace Group*, a small group of artists who work in contemporary lace and put on exhibitions of their work. In 2014 she was among the artists invited to participate in *Imagine...Lace at Waddesdon*, an invitational exhibit held at Waddesdon Manor, a National Trust property in Buckinghamshire.

An interesting facet of Watts' history as a lace artist is her friendship with Ros Hills, also in this exhibit. The two ran "Lace combination courses" together where they encouraged students to combine needle and bobbin lace in contemporary ways. Sometimes they worked collaboratively on a piece. They shared an interest in forging new paths in the use of color and texture.

Denise Watts. *Dried Hydrangea,* 1988-89. Bobbin lace containing 5 areas of collage and hand stitching, 11″ x 9″.

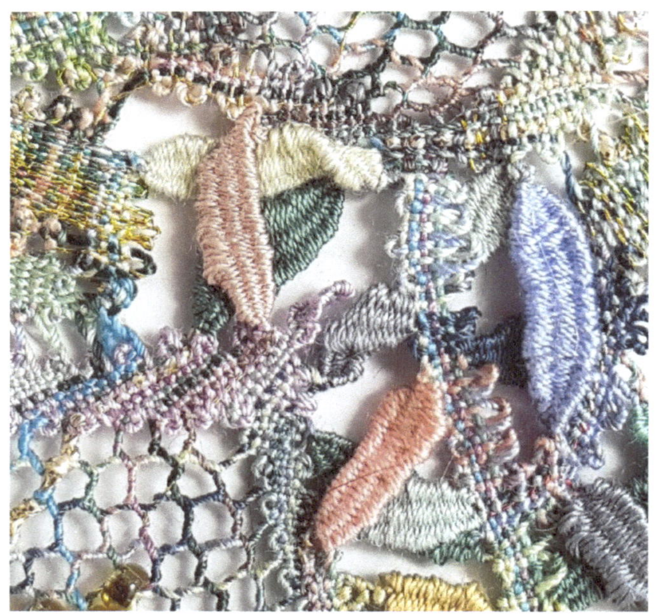

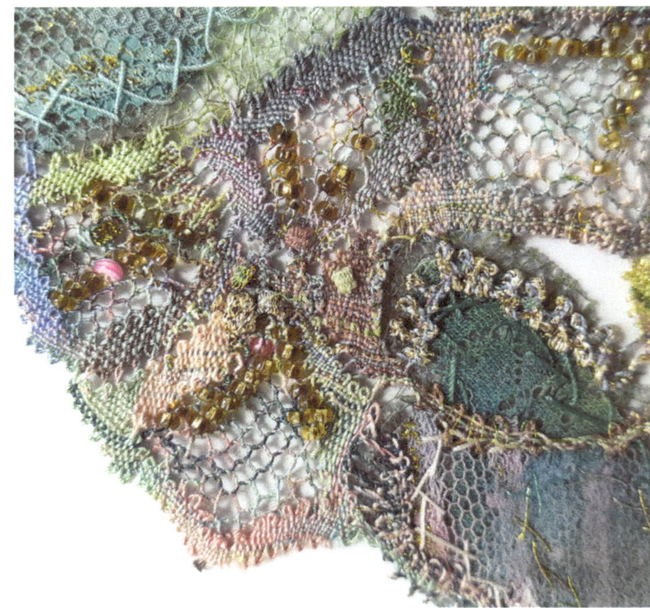

Watts finds historical inspiration in plaited laces, both the earliest plaited laces dating from the 16th century and those of Thomas Lester in the 19th century. She finds that the Lester laces, which are a form of Bedfordshire lace, give definition, shading, form, balance, and texture without limitation and cites them as an influence on *Dried Hydrangea.*

It is easy to see *Dried Hydrangea* as a triumph in color blending, but it is also fascinating from a technical standpoint. Petals (leaf shaped tallies) are structures that take on the color only of the weaving thread while concealing the colors of the passives. Watt's use of this simple concept as she moves colors in and out of the traditional Bedfordshire trails is breath taking. Her petals defy notions of uniformity, much prized in traditional lace, to assume different lengths and shapes. Sometimes bi-colored, sometimes twisted, sometimes overlapping, they form a writhing center to the piece, like a colorful fish pond. The tight single thread weaving of the tallies induces a smooth, reflective sheen, a different impact than the linen stitch or point ground areas. Rolled tallies and beads contribute to the rich texture, as do the applied and layered fabrics held in place with loose impressionistic stitches. Watts's work, emerging from a time when contemporary lace was often derided by traditionalists is truly revolutionary.

I am an artist who has used bobbin lace techniques and equipment to create work since 1979, working with threads of silk, cotton, linen, horsehair, metal, strips of fabric and other non-traditional materials in varying colours and textures. My journey has followed different paths at different times exploring diverse interests.

This work was created while investigating techniques to fabricate form, rhythm, and shading; exploring the interconnections of threads that change the way light falls within the work, thus initiating variation and interest. This became my focus for a while resulting in a collection of small sample works from which Dried Hydrangea developed.

At a time when white traditional lace was being mounted onto squares of equally white cloth as a matter of course, I wanted to re-think the concept of applying lace and fabric together. This work contains five areas of hand dyed collaged fabric, (some of it handmade lace cut up), in the shape of hydrangea flowers. They have then been incorporated into the lace by working into these areas as the piece progressed.

Denise Watts. *Dried Hydrangea.* Color play in tallies. Detail.

Denise Watts. *Dried Hydrangea.* Bobbin lace worked into fabric. Detail.

## Louise West

Louise West is a contemporary lace artist who develops designs based on the traditional English laces of Bedfordshire and Bucks Point. Fascinated by lace history and traditions, she enjoys incorporating references to lace history in her contemporary work. West traces her lacemaking roots and interest in historical lace to a great-great-great-grandmother who was a lacemaker in Northamptonshire. The artist is a graduate of the rigorous and prestigious City and Guilds program in lacemaking. She followed this with a BA in Textile Design and an MA in Art and Design always focusing on lacemaking. Among her achievements is the recently produced book *Bedfordshire Lace Designs.*[59] Working from her studio in Derby, UK, West teaches classes and executes commissioned art.

West is well known for her mastery of Bedfordshire lace, a form of guipure lace that was popular in Britain in the 19th century. She was inspired by the complex designs of Thomas Lester that she studied at the Cecil Higgins Museum in Bedford. Lester's art nouveau lace was excitingly representational and reflective of the 19th century interest in natural history, not only incorporating recognizable plants, but also animals, such as giraffes and ostriches.[60] In 2017 West was asked by the Danish Lace Guild to participate in the making of a gift to celebrate the golden wedding anniversary of Queen Margrethe II and Prince Henrik. She chose to design a panel of English dog roses and daisies inspired by the wild countryside hedgerows interpreted in the spirit of Thomas Lester.[61]

Although she is most closely identified with Bedfordshire lace, West's work *Plant Stems* is based in point ground lace. *Plant Stems* was part of the artist's work for her master's degree and is the culmination of a great deal of historical research as well as contemporary inspiration. Traditional grounds, often considered secondary in lace design, are elevated to primary importance in the wire lace columns. In this case the ground is not the negative space surrounding the motif. Instead it is the focus.

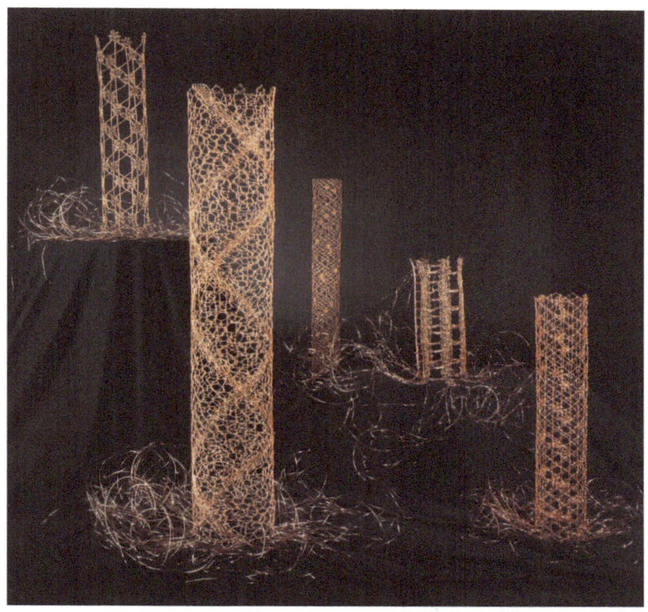

Issues in the contemporary plant world concerning the modification and hybridization of plants, for a bigger and better crop, or for specific characteristics were the inspiration for the piece. The five stems were 'genetically modified' from traditional lace to become bigger and bolder for the 21st century. They incorporate various lace grounds to form the cell structure of the stems, with the largest stem, incorporating the DNA helix containing the essence of lace in the form of rose ground and the support pattern from enlarged plant cell structure. The work is a hybridization of traditional and contemporary, of minor elements becoming the focus, on a larger scale with different materials and yet still having the origins of traditional stitches and botanical roots.

Louise West. *Plant Stems,* 2013. Wire in bobbin lace techniques, 6′ x 4′. Photo: Matthew Jones Photography.

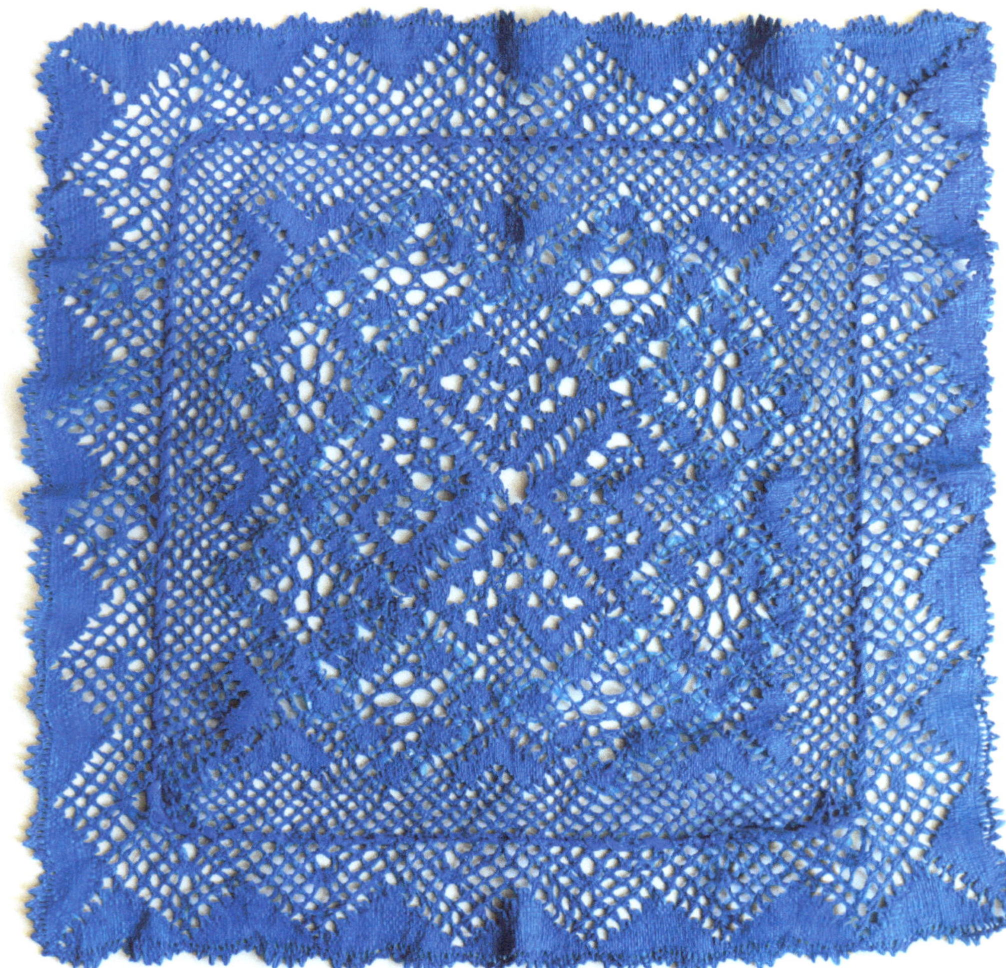

## Ashley Williams

Ashley Williams graduated from the Maryland Institute College of Art with a fiber focus. While there she became intrigued with lace. Since lace instruction was not offered in the fiber program she taught herself the technique from books she borrowed from the library and purchased. She works in Torchon lace, considered a simple, durable lace made on a right-angled grid, and favored for household use.

Moving to Brooklyn exposed Williams to features of urban living such as multiple housemates and the use of the services of commercial laundries. The blue plastic bags from which *Blue Plastic Doily* is constructed were accumulated by her and her fellow residents from the nearby laundromat. As she explains, they "became iconic in our building for clean clothing." *Blue Plastic Doily* was exhibited at *Recycle II* in 2016, a national juried show of "art crafted from cast-off, discarded and re-purposed materials" put on by the Brooklyn Waterfront Artists Coalition.[62] The artist has been active in the lively artistic community of Greenpoint, Brooklyn.

Williams's other lace works, bobbin lace doilies made from black plastic bags, memorialize bodegas and the culture of the corner store.

My work uses traditional craft techniques to transform modern materials into art. Using plastic bags from a corner store or laundromat to construct these bobbin lace doilies exposes the delicate details to a more vivid investigation. Elements such as the stitching, colors, and pattern are then imagined once as the original material, only to be wondered how it was reconstructed. Transforming a material that is usually functional, disposable, small, into something delicate, mesmerizing, and delightfully sizable is my inspiration.

Ashley Williams. *Blue Plastic Doily,* 2014. Bobbin lace produced from plastic bags, 59″ x 59″. Photo: Joshua David McKenney

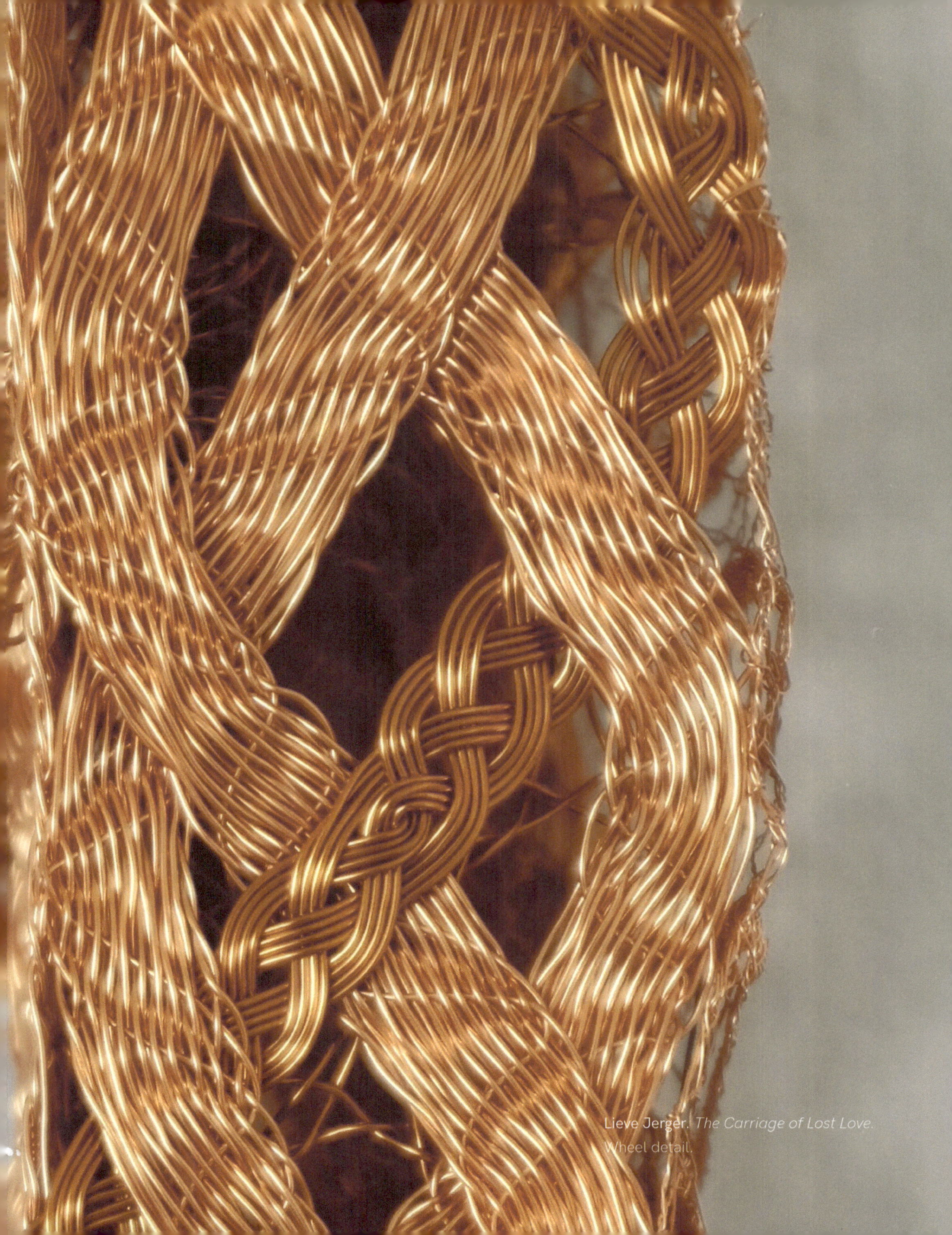

Lieve Jerger. *The Carriage of Lost Love.* Wheel detail.

## Endnotes

[1] Smolková, Marie A. a Regina BÍBOVÁ. "Krajky a krajkářství lidu slovanského v Čechách, na Moravě, ve Slezsku a uh. Slovensku". Praha: Nákladem vlastním (Self published), 1908.

[2] Kaethe Kliot and her husband Jules are seminal figures in American lace. Their store Lacis in Berkeley served as a source for lace tools and materials. Now it also houses a museum of lace begun in honor of Kaethe by her husband Jules. Her book published in 1973 was a major influence on the US lace revival of the 1970s. (Kliot)

[3] (Cook and Stott)

[4] (Yeh and Jerger)

[5] An excellent resource about Slovenian lace is Idrija Lace: A History Written in Thread (Leskovec and Terpin)

[6] The Women's Institute was founded in 1915 to revitalize rural communities and encourage women to become more involved in producing food during WWI. A nationwide women's organization, it has sought to provide women with educational opportunities and the chance to build new skills.(The Women's Institute)

[7] (Atkinson)

[8] (Atkinson, Contemporary Lace for You)

[9] Continuous lace is worked in a strip with the same number of threads throughout, moving between the motifs and background. Part lace is worked in sections and joined with sewings.

[10] Ebb'n'Flow: Lace, Place and Climate, Sept. 15- Oct. 28th, 2018 at Walford Mill Crafts, Wimborne U.K., and Priest's House Museum, Wimborne U.K.

[11] (Banatova, Art of Bobbin Lace)

[12] (Banatova, Internet discussion in Contemporary Lace group)

[13] (Banatova, Art of Bobbin Lace)

[14] http://choishine.com/TheLaceConcept.html

[15] http://www2.cs.arizona.edu/patterns/weaving/books/dmc_lace_1.pdf

[16] (Nordfors)

[17] (Smith)

[18] (de Dillmont)

[19] (Caulfeild and Saward)

[20] (J. and P. Coats Ltd)

[21] (Clark)

[22] (Clark 125)

[23] Eremiášová appeared in an important show of Czech lace artists at the Musées royaux d'Art et d'Histoire in 1983. (Houart)

[24] (Halíková 108-109)

[25] In the 1990s Ulrike Löhr taught a class in designing grounds. This ground, B 119 appeared in the third of a series of 4 compilations of grounds, largely taken from historical lace, that Löhr began to release in 2002 as packets of pages to be put in a loose-leaf binder. This series was called Viele Gute Gründe. (Löhr)

[26] The first publication of what was to become a popular mainstay of contemporary bobbin lace, "chaos ground" was by Ulrike Löhr in 1991. (Löhr 33)

[27] Macramé enjoyed a great deal of popularity during the craft revival of the 1970s, possibly setting the stage for a revival of bobbin lacemaking. For a history of Macramé see (Gwynne 110-111)

[28] For a fascinating description of lace villages in the English Midlands see the book Lace Villages. (Bartlett)

[29] (Southard)

[30] (Stott and Cook 42,52)

[31] The pricking is an actual size template providing a pin placement guide. The lace is made on the pricking.

[32] The Lace Dealer's Pattern Book is a book of small samples of Buckinghamshire and Bedfordshire lace

probably used to show customers laces that they might order. It was acquired by the Wardown Park Museum in Luton in 1955 and its provenance is from a Miss F.E. Haines the last proprietor of a firm built and run by Thomas Lester and his sons. It may also have belonged to John Spencer (1830-1895) another local lace dealer. The book was considered so significant that when the museum sought funds for its restoration in 1994, the Lacemaker's Circle and the Arachne internet group launched a fund-raising appeal. This resulted in its restoration, and the subsequent publication of a reproduction by the Friends of the Luton Museum in 1998 and 2012. (Roseground)

[33] (Aemilia Ars) (Museo Davia Bargellini) (Bernardini, Poli and Baldi) (Il Punto Antico)

[34] Powerhouse Museum, A5335. Lace panel, "Judith and Holofernes", needle lace, linen / silk / human hair, maker unknown, England, mid 1600s https://ma.as/183127

[35] Metropolitan Museum of Art, 09.68.90. Panel, 16th-17th century, needle lace, punto in aria. Purchase by subscription, 1909.

[36] (Emőke, Emese and Aurél 40)This book is very informative about Halas Lace. See also (Halas Lace Catalogue) (Earnshaw)

[37] Victoria and Albert Museum, T. 131-1986. Purse, Ros Hills, needle lace, 1986.

[38] (Hills)

[39] (Earnshaw, Merehurst Embroidery Skills: Needlelace 120)

[40] (Hills and Gibson, Needlelace Stitches)

[41] For a concise diagram of the possibilities, see (Hills, Colour and Texture in Needlelace 78)

[42] (Irvine)

[43] (Irvine and Ruskey, Developing a Mathematical Model for Bobbin Lace)

[44] (Powerhouse Museum 79, 186)

[45] For a perceptive discussion of Millerson's work, see (McElroy)

[46] (Grimwood)

[47] A 19th and early 20th century Belgian needle lace with a springy background mesh and widely spaced cordonette stitches.

[48] (Griswold and Parrish) The Digital Archive of Documents related to Lace is the labor of love of Professor Ralph Griswold and Tess Parrish. Griswold, a computer scientist who was the originator of several early computer languages, became fascinated with weaving because it is binary like computers. In retirement he began to collect and scan documents related to weaving to share on the internet. Tess Parrish, a lacemaker, collaborated with him by scanning documents related to lace with the assistance of many members of the lace community.

[49] (Cole 45) (Palliser 417)

[50] For a fascinating description of this industry see (Tomlinson)

[51] (Woods)

[52] (Powerhouse Museum 122-123,162-163,195)

[53] (Powerhouse Museum 125, 195)

[54] (G. Stott)

[55] (Rixon)

[56] (Powerhouse Museum 129, 196)

[57] This award, given by the Textile Society of America honors Joanne Siegal Brandford who often used lace techniques in her textile art. It is very appropriate that it was given to Valentine, a lace artist.

[58] https://www.design.iastate.edu/awards/olivia-valentine-2/

[59] (Stillwell 215)

[60] (West)

[61] (Buck 71-72)

[62] (West, The English Hedgerows)

[63] http://bwac.org/2015/11/recycle-2016/

## Glossary

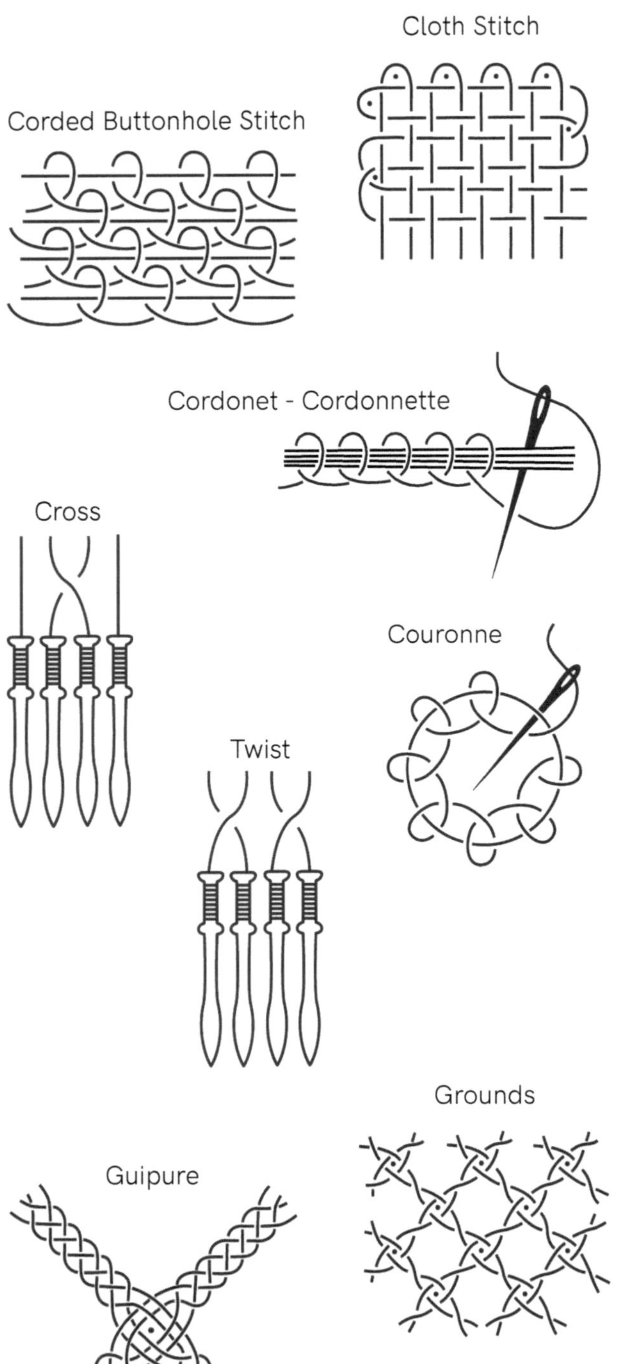


**Cloth stitch** – In bobbin lace, a stitch that resembles woven cloth in appearance.

**Corded buttonhole stitch / corded Brussels stitch** – A buttonhole stitch that is worked over a straight thread having the effect of making the buttonhole stitch larger and more opaque.

**Cordonet** – Padding laid along the edges of needle lace motifs to emphasize the shape by making the edges more prominent.

**Cordonnette** – In needle lace, stitching over the cordonet which holds it in place, covers it, and creates the opportunity for more embellishment.

**Couronne** – A circle of thread covered in buttonhole stitch applied to the surface of lace to create a three-dimensional embellishment.

**Cross and twist** – The two basic stitches in bobbin lace.

**Grounds** – The background stitches that fill the areas between motifs, and sometimes inside motifs.

**Guipure** – Lace where the motifs are connected by bars instead of a mesh.

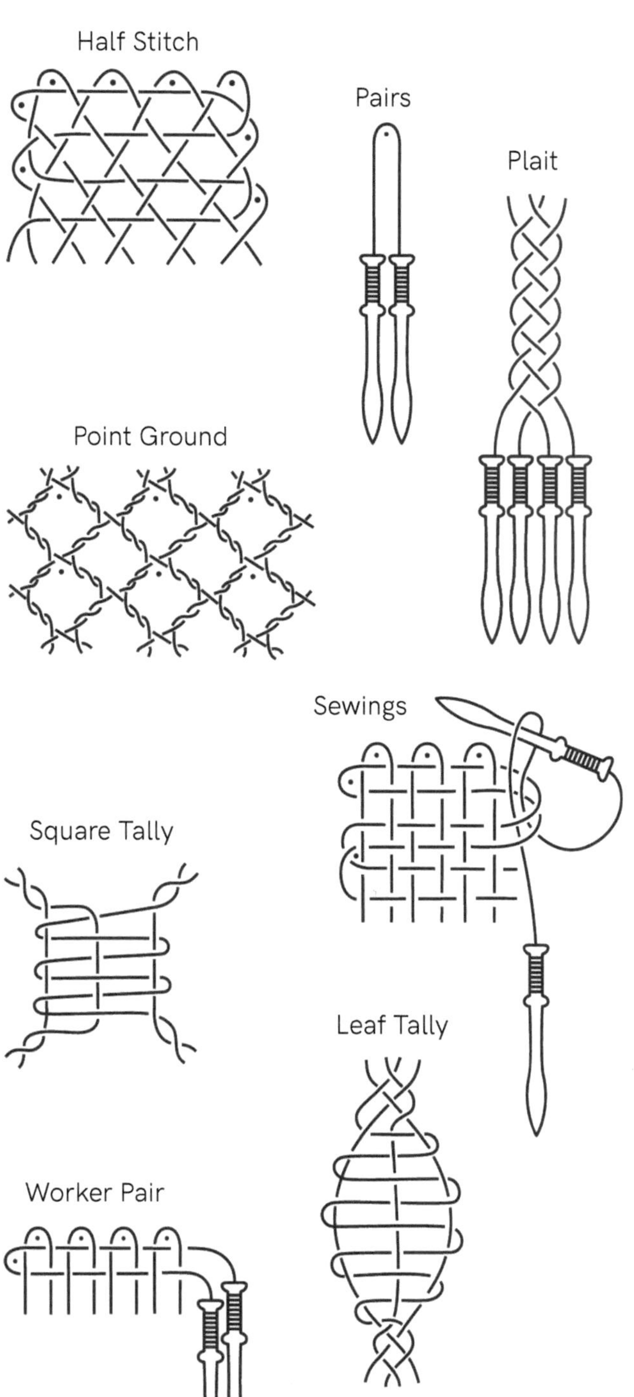


**Half stitch** – In bobbin lace, a stitch made by crossing and twisting the threads which has the appearance of lines separated by Xs.

**Pairs** – In bobbin lace, the minimum working unit is not a single thread but a pair of threads.

**Passive pair** – In bobbin lace, a pair that is functioning at a particular moment as the warp.

**Plait** – A four strand braid.

**Point ground** – Point ground lace became popular in the 19th century. It is a light ground of crosses and twists without the braided connections that characterized laces such as Mechlin in the 18th century.

**Sewings** – In bobbin lace, especially part lace, different areas are attached to each other by a maneuver in which the thread of one bobbin is pulled through the lace with a crochet hook forming a loop. The other threaded bobbin passes through the loop and both are tightened forming a secure join.

**Tally** – In bobbin lace, the tally is formed of four threads, two pairs. One thread acts as a weft weaving back and forth across the other three, forming a structure that is usually square or leaf shaped.

**Worker pair** – In bobbin lace, a pair that is functioning at a particular moment as a weft.

# Bibliography


Aemilia Ars. Merletti E Ricami della Aemilia Ars. Ed. Elisa Ricci. University Press, Bologna, 1999. Milan: Casa Editrice d'Arte Bestetti & Tumminelli, 1929.

Atkinson, Jane. Contemporary Lace for You. Christchurch, Dorset, UK: Webfoot Books, 2011.

—. Pattern Design for Torchon Lace. London: B.T. Batsford Ltd, 1987.

Banatova, Daniela. Art of Bobbin Lace. 2006. <http://danielabanatova.webs.com/>.

—. laceioli.ning.com. January-February 2013. <http://laceioli.ning.com/group/contemporary-bobbin-lace/forum/topics/work-of-daniela-banatova>.

Bartlett, Liz. Lace Villages. London: B.T. Batsford Ltd, 1991.

Bernardini, Carla, Doretta Davanzo Poli and Orsola Ghetti Baldi. Aemilia Ars: Arts & Crafts a Bologna, 1898-1903. Bologna: A+G Edizioni, 2001.

Buck, Anne. Thomas Lester, his Lace and the East Midlands Industry, 1820-1905. Carlton: Ruth Bean, 1981.

Caulfeild, Sophia Frances and Blanche C. Saward. The Dictionary of Needlework, Facsimile of the 1882 edition. New York: Arno Press, 1972.

Clark, Jill Nordfors. Needle Lace: Techniques and Inspiration. Tunbridge Wells, Kent: Search Press Limited, 1999.

Cole, Alan S. A supplemental descriptive catalogue of specimens of lace acquired for the South Kensington museum between 1880 and June 1890. H.M. Stationery Office, 1891.

Cook, Bridget and Geraldine Stott. The Book of Bobbin Lace Stitches. London: B.T. Batsford, 1980.

de Dillmont, Thérèse. The Complete Encyclopedia of Needlework. Mulhouse, France: Dollfus Mieg & Cie, 1884.

Earnshaw, Pat. Merehurst Embroidery Skills: Needlelace. Reprint of 1991 edition. London: Merehurst Limited, 1992.

—. Outlines and Stitches: A Guide to Design, with special reference to Halas Needlelaces. Guildford: Gorse Publications, 1992.

Emőke, Láslo, Pásztor Emese and Szakál Aurél. Halas Lace (Halasi Csipke). Kiskunhalas: Halasi Csipe Alapítvány, 1996.

Grimwood, Valerie. Starting Needlepoint Lace. London: B.T. Batsford, 1989.

Griswold, Ralph and Tess Parrish. The Digital Archive of Documents Related to Lace. Comps. Ralph Griswold and Tess Parrish. n.d. Electronic. 28 June 2018. <https://www2.cs.arizona.edu/patterns/weaving/lace.html>.

Gwynne, Judith L. The Illustrated Dictionary of Lace. London: B.T. Batsford Ltd, 1997.

Halas Lace Catalogue. Kiskunhalas: Halasi Csipe Alapítvány, Unknown, after 1997.

Halíková, Anna. Milča Eremiášová: Řeč Krajky. Prague: Česká palička, 2002.

Hills, Ros and Pat Gibson. Needlelace Stitches. London: B.T. Batsford, 1989.

Hills, Ros. Colour and Texture in Needlelace. London: Dryad Press, 1987.

Houart, Charles. La Dentelle Tchèque: De L'Art Déco à nos jours. Brussels : Communaute francaise de Belgigue, 1983.

Il Punto Antico. Aemilia Ars: Desegni E Merletti, designs and lace. Bologna: Il Punto Antico, 2007.

Irvine, Veronika and Frank Ruskey. "Developing a Mathematical Model for Bobbin Lace." Journal of Mathematics and the Arts 8.No. 3-4 (2014): 95-110. 28 June 2018. <https://arxiv.org/abs/1406.1532>.

Irvine, Veronika. "Lace Tessellations: A mathematical model for bobbin lace and an exhaustive combinatorial search for patterns." 2016. 28 June 2018. <http://dspace.library.uvic.ca/handle/1828/7495>.

J. and P. Coats Ltd. Anchor Manual of Needlework. London: B. T. Batsford Ltd, 1958.

Kliot, Kaethe and Jules. Bobbin Lace: Form by the Twisting of Cords . New York: Crown Publishers, Inc., 1973.

Leskovec, Ivana and Marija Terpin. Idrija Lace, A History Written in Thread. 2nd. Idrija: Mestni muzej Idrijac, 2013.

Löhr, Ulrike. Schmetterlinge: 10 Kloppelbriefe. Dortmund: Self-published, 1991.

Löhr, Ulrike. Viele Gute Grunde. Bochum: Self-published, 2002. Loose leaves.

McElroy, Gil. "Dorie Millerson: The Ties that Bind." Surface Design Spring 2011: 26-29.

Museo Davia Bargellini. Aemilia Ars: Dai vecchi desegni ai nuovi merletti. Bologna: Il Punto Antico, 2008.

Nordfors, Jill Denny. Needle Lace & Needleweaving: A New Look at Traditional Stitches. New York: Van Nostrand Reinhold Company, 1974.

Palliser, Mrs. Bury. History of Lace. Ed. Margaret Jourdain. Dover edition, an unabridged republication of the edition published by Charles Scribner's Sons in 1911. Mineola: Dover Publications, 1984.

Powerhouse Museum. Love Lace: Powerhouse Museum, International Lace Award. Ed. Lindie Ward. Sydney: Powerhouse Publishing, 2011.

Rixon, Angharad Louise. Raising the Profile of Lace: 1st International Symposiumof Young Lace Makers. Pavia: Self published by Textile Support, 2013.

Roseground, a complete lacemaker to lacemaker service. n.d. electronic. 27 June 2018. <https://www.roseground.com/books/lacemaking-books/the-lace-dealerus-pattern-book>.

Smith, Barbara Lee. "Gut Responses, A Conversation with Jill Nordfors Clark." Surface Design Spring 2017: 22-26.

Southard, Doris. Bobbin Lacemaking. Paper back edition. Originally published in 1977. New York: Charles Scribner's Sons, 1983.

Stillwell, Alexandra. Cassell Illustrated Dictionary of Lacemaking. London: Cassell Publishers Ltd, 1996.

Stott, Geraldin. The Bobbin Lace Manual. London: B.T. Batsford Ltd, 2002.

Stott, Geraldine and Bridget Cook. 100 Traditional Bobbin Lace Patterns. New York: Larousse & Co., Inc, 1982.

The Women's Institute. The WI: Inspiring Women. n.d. Electronic. 26 June 2018. <www.thewi.org.uk/about-the-wi >.

Tomlinson, Margaret. Three Generations in the Honiton Lace Trade. Sidmouth: Self published, Sovereign Printing Group, 1985.

West, Louise. Bedfordshire Lace Designs. Exeter: Short Run Press, Ltd, 2017.

—. "The English Hedgerows." The Bulletin: International Organization of Lace, Inc. Winter 2018.

Woods, Sandi. Special Effects in Bobbin Lace. London: B.T. Batsford Ltd, 1998.

Yeh, Phil and Lieve Jerger. The Winged Tiger and the Lace Princess. Kailua, Hawaii: Hawaya, 1998.

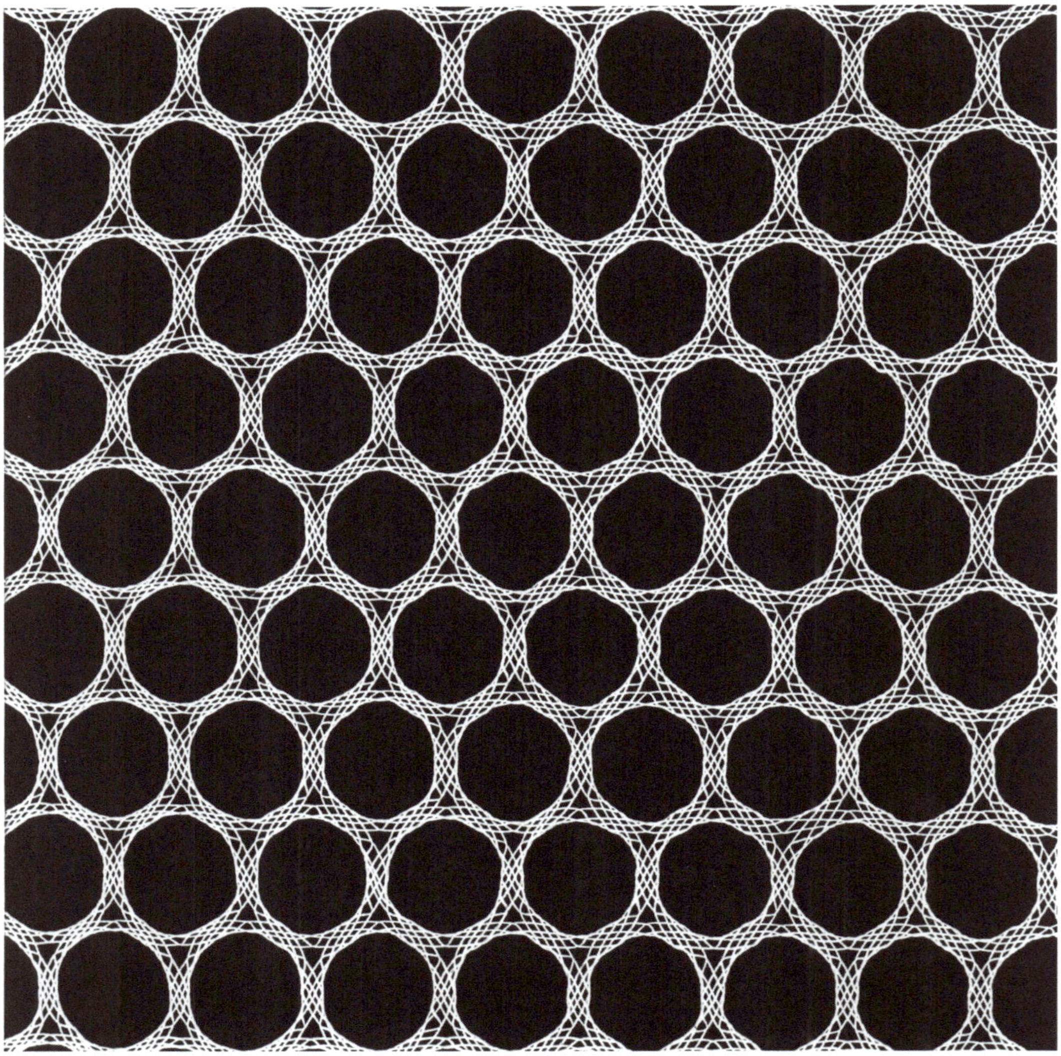

Veronika Irvine. *Bee Prepared,* 2015, White cotton thread on charcoal raw silk, handmade bobbin lace, 12″ x 12″.

The exhibition Lace not Lace: Contemporary Fiber Art from Lacemaking Techniques is generously supported by The Coby Foundation, Ltd. and the International Organization of Lace, Inc. Museum programs are made possible by funds from the New Jersey State Council on the Arts, a partner agency of the National Endowment for the Arts, the Geraldine R. Dodge Foundation, and other corporations, foundations, and individuals.

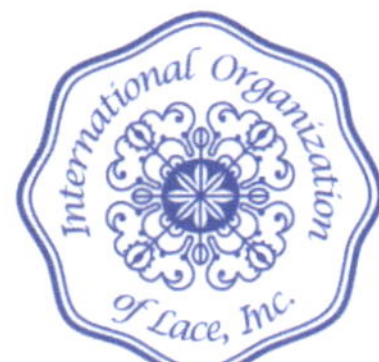

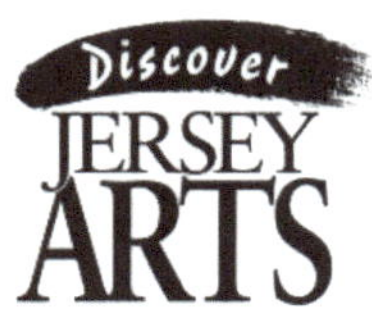

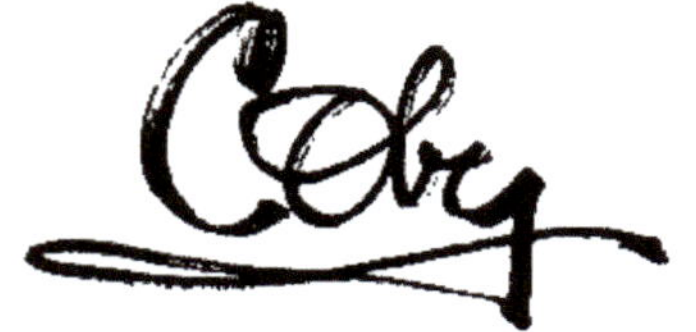

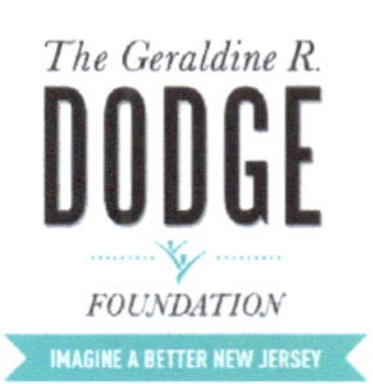

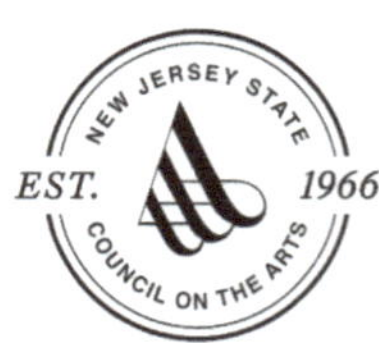

www.ingramcontent.com/pod-product-compliance
Lightning Source LLC
LaVergne TN
LVHW070218110826
845147LV00003B/602
*9781732622401*